# *Morning Light*

## The Spiritual Journal of Jean Sulivan

Jean Sulivan

*Translated by Joseph Cunneen*
*and Patrick Gormally*

Paulist Press
*New York / Mahwah*

The translators express their gratitude to Mercy College and to the Maynooth Scholastic Trust and the Publication Committee for their assistance in the preparation of this work.

*Book design by Nighthawk Design.*

Originally published in French as *Matinales,* copyright ©1976 by Editions Gallimard. English translation copyright ©1988 by The Missionary Society of St. Paul the Apostle in the State of New York.

Library of Congress Cataloging-in-Publication Data

Sulivan, Jean.
[Matinales.   English]
Morning light: the spiritual journal of Jean Sulivan/Jean
Sulivan; translated by Joseph Cunneen.
p.   cm.
Translation of: Matinales.
ISBN 0-8091-2985-X (pbk.) : $12.95 (est.)
1. Spiritual life—Catholic authors.   2. Sulivan, Jean.
I. Title.
BX2350.2.S7913   1988
248.4'82—dc19. 88-18769 CIP

Published by Paulist Press
997 Macarthur Boulevard
Mahwah, New Jersey 07430

Printed and bound in the
United States of America

# WORD

IT HAD TO BE mother who passed on the heritage to me, she who had nothing else to leave, just as her parents had passed it on to her. In her house the father used to read the Old and the New Testament aloud every winter evening, and even the dogs didn't dare move.

Today television reigns. Ecclesiastics, looking humble and contrite, sometimes appear on it, or some professional popularizer—an ex-prophet who blabbers about psychoanalysis, sex, morality, education, no matter what. It's been a long time now since we entered the desert of the soul. And our official guides only enlarge it with ideas, theories and debates from the passing parade of religion and spectacle.

Mother knew by heart the stories of Abraham, Moses, Ruth and Tobit, the psalms, each parable, the curses in chapter 23 of Matthew.

It had to be my mother.

"Of all that has been written, I love what is written in blood. Write in blood and you will learn that blood is spirit," wrote Friedrich Nietzsche.

We were poor like the peasants of India or Palestine, and joyful because we were part of something. There was no shame then in being poor. The thousand stings of desire and vanity were foreign to us. Today all we have are poor people who have not yet succeeded in getting rich. Mother, each Sunday after vespers, walked by herself around the fields, fingering her rosary, and observed the swellings of spring, the whitening harvests, the bareness of winter.


The Gospel emerged from a world of peasants and sailors. Jesus is the rabbi whose word is transpierced with images of trees, water, harvests, cattle, shepherds and vagabonds. As if there were a secret connection between the earth, that which presses against it and the invisible. I know very well how old-fashioned and reactionary these ideas are, especially after Rudolf Bultmann and Emmanuel Levinas. So what? I, too, believe in the necessity of uprooting. But surely it is first necessary to have had roots, to have felt the earth's heartbeat. It seems to me many of our current intellectual masters speak about everywhere, and nowhere.

Beggars used to pass by our house and sleep in our barn, after putting their matches on the table. We knew their names and what it was to share a bit of bread, a glass of milk, a bowl of soup. They were part of us.

It is obvious Jesus lives in the depths of non-duality—that is, where God, the other, and ourselves form only one reality. This is my body, this is my blood.

## Good-Bye to Nostalgia

Nevertheless, I left, with enthusiasm, the world of villages for the big town, like the first imbecile who happened by, because there was no longer any place in it for me. I don't regret it. Good-bye to nostalgia. People should stop talking about the anonymity of cities. We don't know our neighbors in the next apartment—so then what? Hurrah for freedom, and an end to hypocrisy. In cities people get together with those they choose; such meetings are more true, as brief as life.

Yes, large towns were always accursed—it says so all through the Bible. Condemned to endless wandering, Cain invented the town as a substitute for Eden. Cain and his posterity. That's why towns are accursed. Babylon and Nineveh, like the cities on the edge of the lake. Jerusalem itself. For they are all tied to a greed that is never satisfied, to power—that is, to war. So, sooner or later, they perish by arms or by fire. But ultimately God accepts the human project. The town, just like Jerusalem, becomes the image and promise of the holy city of the Apocalypse, which "has no need for the sun and the moon to shine, for the glory of God has illumined it!"

Surrounded by concrete, many of us carry our village within us as a joyful wound, where the primordial word remains a ferment. We are secret combatants, spies for both sides. Sometimes we even seem like traitors.


## Lost in a Forest of Ideas

Mother knew by heart the words she spoke in a light, swaying rhythm. I watched her eyes, her lips, her gestures; I heard her breathing: Look at the birds of the air. They do not sow nor do they harvest, nor do they gather into barns. . . . Carry neither gold nor silver nor money in your girdles. . . . There was a sower who went out to sow. . . . A man had two sons. . . . Jerusalem, Jerusalem, you who kill the prophets. . . .

I didn't understand the meaning. In every poem the revelation is not situated only, or primarily, in the idea; it is not a knowledge. It is born of a breathing and a rhythm—that is to say, it is conveyed by the body, and not only by the mind. It wasn't until I discovered a book by Marcel Jousse one day that I had the courage to speak out of my own experience, overcoming the natural horror I had of talking directly about religion.

Then there had been school, college, priests. Innocently carried along by the customs and thought patterns of the group, careful to

4

communicate a possession, a knowledge which would give them power, they made use of the Gospel. As if it were a sermon, and not first of all the Word springing up in the night of conscience. No more rhythmic breathing, the death of the poem. Instead, a coherent construction, falsely reasonable, of ideas and principles.

What happened keeps on happening, endlessly. How much time do we need to understand it? The scribes and the high priests live in us, in you, in me, and they never lay down their arms. Just as Jesus was rejected, tracked down and killed out of fidelity to God, in the same way, out of fidelity to the message, his Word has been hardened—"ossified," as the Jesuit anthropologist would say—by the very ones whose mission it was to announce it. *They know not what they do.*

They made use of the Gospel, read once and for all, it seemed, in order to prove that Jesus was the Son of God, that he had risen again, that the Church had been founded by him, that everything had been established, once and for all. That's what I wanted, too; I had no objection. The only problem was that I felt a deadly boredom. The illusion had been in believing that it was possible to detach an abstract truth from the body of the Word, something which would only involve the head, and in which joy would no longer beat its wings.

They made use of it, too, it is true, in order to make us love Jesus. They made up an image of Jesus that was sometimes sweet and humble, sometimes muscular, depending on the period, sometimes that of a bloodless being with a halo, beyond the spheres. Our teachers were so deprived of elementary psychology that they did not recognize the traps of sentimental exaggeration. When they talked about Jesus, they were generally talking about something else and about their own unhappiness. How would I be able to find fault with them when for so long I allowed myself to be caught in the same trap?

## *I Excelled in Theology*

I never quite fitted in. After first showing some stubbornness—out of some healthy instinct—I trained myself to act like others. I wrote term papers giving the right answers, I applied myself in Greek and Hebrew, I excelled in theology. I loved truth, got carried away, went through a pious period, letting everything else go. I told God, "You are my rock." Someone who has not experienced this satisfaction of spirit, this metaphysical eroticism, this aura of peace separating one from the real body of life, will never have an idea of that fabrication we call the interior life.

There were several Madame Bovary types in my seminary, who helped me to see myself as I really was. Some were snapped up by the first girl who came along: they thought they had lost their faith, betrayed their vocation. But these are just words. Others, sheltered in the cocoon of a closed intellectualism and religiosity, moved on into the field of their ambition. Abstract and sentimental piety fits in quite well with conformism and the passion to succeed, which can take on a mystic coloration.

I also met some pious men in my seminary, stamped with a different piety, lucid and critical, like flaming coals.

Let's stop a second. How many men were there whom I could think of as brothers of the Son of Man? Those who made fine declarations of their zeal, the official defenders of the faith, fanatics of the past who were neurotic about the future? Or the suicidally dedicated, specialists, for example, in the audiovisual field, born to sacralize everything in appearance, while opening up the road to atheism? The eternal organizers, businessmen in the service of the supposedly efficient structures of salvation? Overextended intellectuals who shut themselves up in conceptual palaces, whether ancient or modern? No, I saw them only too eagerly following their natural bent. What they called faith was the strength that resided in them, their unused natural energies.

So, how many were brothers? A few. But that's enough for fraternity. It was these who formed me, helped me get past appearances. Men without too much vanity or ambition, who could look serenely at death and know how to laugh.

Brothers and sisters who meet together in truth—that's the Church. The rest is only a big, necessary apparatus which fulfills its function when it permits them to live in communion. The empire doesn't interest me. I accept the remains of empire provided that something is stirring inside it, the creative liberty of men and women wounded by the Gospel.

The day came when I gave lectures, taught courses, delivered sermons, hoping both to express a few truths that had become mine, and also to please, to protect myself by offering a mixture of boldness and teasing. I became expert in the art of holding back what I was giving. Because it was necessary to watch out. An audience wants to recognize what it already knows. They like to be stirred up, but as little as necessary. Except for a small number, they haven't come to search for the Word. Woe to you if you attack their certitudes head-on—that is, the truths they're accustomed to or their interests.

Why act surprised? It's the order of things, and not just in the religious field. Under Pius XII, if I had announced the Word boldly, I would have suffered. What a pity! With the halo of a martyr, I would have been able, like many others, to install myself in a new conformism, all the while believing that I was still on the front line. To be honest, what held me back was less cowardice than the clear awareness that at the bottom of my oratorical outbursts, there was resentment and the desire to show off. When you see a great speaker step forward from among those prominent in today's media circus, you know he's not going to proclaim the Word.

Yesterday, as still today, it was necessary to please the political and religious hierarchies who offered you their hand—a heavier hand yesterday than today. The hierarchy proper had, it believed, to take into account many things. It was a little cross-eyed. One eye was on the tiny fringe of the faithful who surrounded the bishops and prevented them from seeing the crowd; another was on Rome, which insisted that the Word be preached but was no longer open to conversion by it, because Rome itself had a monopoly on all its meanings.

Therefore I spouted a kind of finicky oratory. I attacked laziness and indifference. I felt I was a true believer, inspired in the pulpit. Afterward, I became as gloomy as a fish. . . . How many times have I wanted to surrender myself again to eloquence—it is such a drug. But it was no longer possible.

In short, during my active service as a priest, I have assisted and participated in the humiliation of the Word, both within me and outside me, to the profit of ideologies and sentiments.

## To Write In Order To Lie Less

One could laugh at certain questions that have become deliciously popular these days, but finally, when something happened that woke me up, it was this. Only one question in my head: Who is speaking, from where, to whom? I had only been repeating what I had been taught and was experiencing an inner weariness. When was I only a reflection of my environment, and when was I speaking in my own voice? It was impossible and pointless to try to answer. As soon as I became conscious of this uncertainty, no longer knowing who I was, when I was preaching the Gospel or when a certain kind of cleverness was helping me say what was appropriate, the idea came to me to leave the Church.

But to go where? Especially since I had no special urge to be a link in the human chain; the species had no need of me. For some reason or other, I was marked by the absolute, the Gospel. There would have

7

been a lot of hypocrisy in leaving and slamming the door, or in asking for reduction to the lay state, as they put it, under the pretext that the Church did not conform to the idea I had made of it out of the Scripture and tradition it had communicated to me.

Besides, once out of adolescence, I had never believed the Church was about to present a perfect image of the kingdom. On the contrary, I believe the ultimate destiny of the world is being played out in the battle that takes place within the Church and outside it, between the Church and the Word; it is to the degree that it battles against its own sclerosis that it is a light to the world.

If I tried to be free of all priestly responsibilities—and was able to be, thanks to the perhaps skeptical benevolence of a cardinal—it was not to place myself at a distance, but to be present in a different fashion.

To write is to enter into silence, to speak in a low voice for the few who enter into silence with you because they recognize a voice that is rising up out of themselves. There exists a race of people, you see, who are in harmony with you. One is a writer, another is a reader, what does it matter? They are branches of the same stream, beyond ideas and opinions. If so many human beings live by appearances and exhaust themselves in the theater of the world, it is in order to cover over the depth of the abyss. For if the immemorial voice continued to murmur to them, they would no longer be able to believe in progress, money, success or glory.

Writing isn't what people think it to be: arranging one's ideas outside oneself in terms of a logic that carries with it the consent of the mind. Such a process could unfold only within the framework of an already accepted body of knowledge. That's the way professional thinkers and commentators operate. But to write is to forget, to allow memory to become flesh until there emerges the millennial word of that instant which is also eternity—that is, that glimmering of life and death when they meet between the nothingness of the past and the night of that which is to come.

To write is to set out, rejecting the language of the tribe, enrooting oneself elsewhere. Hence it is necessary for the writer to consent to become a stranger, to forget what he knows, or thinks he knows, to run the risk of losing his friends, to not be afraid *to lose his audience* just when he begins to have one.

So I began to write, writing of everything except directly of God, Jesus or faith. I told stories in which lived experience intersected with the imaginary, wounds with joys. I wanted so badly to cleanse myself of formalism, to be cured of taboos and guilt feelings. I tried to provide a passageway for a Word that never left me in peace. I was tied to it, married to it, indissolubly. It didn't prove anything. Was it a matter of new seeds or just left-overs? Was I only the place where my scars expressed themselves, or was there passing through me a breathing that arose from our common anthropological roots? First I thought one thing, then another. But one day I resolved to place my confidence in that Word—which did not seem sure of itself or very glorious, but was nevertheless joyful—in the poverty of an active and passionate doubt that was, I believe, the form of love.

## Why Say I?

I don't believe I write because of the need to share secrets. I prefer to tell stories, to give emphasis to a narrator and some characters while I watch from backstage. My personal journal is mixed in with my books. My preference would be to speak neither about faith nor about myself, but of men and women who set out against the night, of highways and skyscrapers, of the rejects of society, of love, its wounds and cures, in the secret hope that the absolute would offer a sign in spite of me. But many readers, including believers, have written to say that my books have helped them go on living. It is for them that I am writing this. A line of Bernanos has always haunted me: "The writer is only the steward and dispenser of goods that don't belong to him. . . . If he fails in that duty he is less than a dog."

Why say I? It may be only because a deeper knowledge of a writer's subjectivity is liberating for others, encouraging them to become joyously what they are. But also because of a forgotten truth.

To restrict oneself to ideas without ever referring to oneself is nonsense. Yet that's what many thinkers do, never committing themselves. They want us to believe that in the moral and spiritual order there is a logic of ideas that goes on apart from living experience. A humility that consists of not speaking about oneself while identifying with great ideas is the worst kind of pride.

Nevertheless, I must confess, I, too, have often had the temptation to write my book on *Faith* or *The Future of Christianity* from the outside. How peaceful it would be to become invisible behind the smooth pane of the writing, to play with ideas and show how they all fit together while letting the reader think that everything has taken place in a purely impersonal realm. A fine deception. It's what specialists do who build intellectual structures from which they pretend to be absent. Which is why they never finish gabbing about "the crisis of our times" or dream about the future instead of speaking to us directly.

That kind of speaking can only be in the singular. Don't be fooled by it. The person who agrees to reveal his deepest self withdraws into the humility of anonymity even though, at the very moment he detaches himself from the *I* that is naturally social, people think he is an exhibitionist.

In our society, to consent to live out one's difference is to become a rebel, someone who rejects "automatic" attitudes. Do we have to listen to rebels? After all, they're often one-sided and unfair. Why don't they let us get ahead in this world, or at least relieve our boredom before we arrive at the peace of the grave? Even when they recognize the necessity of social forms, they get annoyed if the actors, like spectators, forget there's a show going on. Because they've removed themselves from the game, perhaps simply because they were unskillful at it, they never stop overcompensating for the fact. They bore us with their purity; we know what it's made of. Do we have to listen to rebels? But those who believe in grandeur, prestige and success, who inhabit the world of glory and injustice—are such men in a better position to speak of Jesus?

Have you noticed? Pompous words seem to go along with official dress, with ornaments and decorations, even when those who wear them in ceremonies are themselves poor. It is impossible not to grasp the contradiction between the speech of Jesus and ecclesiastical phraseology, mitres, capes—the whole show. That's not a judgment but an observation. It's jarring. One begins to pity the solemn actors in these ceremonial conferences, as well as the contemporary apostles of encounter groups who are so skillful at manipulating moods, at playing on the saxophone or violin of sentiment. One feels like laughing.

## Return to the Gospel

I was an emigré from within, absent from the rituals, spectacles and debates, from the whole "crisis." There had been a long and secret disaffection in my life during which I'd been busy directing a film club and had gone on several long trips without ever succeeding in hiding a certain emptiness inside me.

The moment can come when everything irritates us: To hear that God exists or that he doesn't, that Jesus is Son of God and is risen or that he isn't, that the Church is in a state of mortal sin or that it's holy, that it ought to get politically involved or ought not, that priests should be able to marry or women become priests. And when you hear prayer used as a medication, a kind of yoga, by some fashionable spiritual director, you feel like saying that the spiritual life is just another product, like a washing machine or new car.

There's no longer a common vocabulary. You're speaking an unknown language whose first word you haven't yet learned. You get the idea that you might as well lapse into the stupidest conformism, become a cynic, go to a large open-air Mass at the football stadium and laugh at the whole thing. In that case you may be on the road to spiritual recovery.

Sometimes I had a presentiment of what affected me. I had traveled in the Middle East, India, and Africa and was familiar with Meister Eckhart, Angelus Silesius, the Tao, the Tch'an. "Superstitions, taboos, values, and everything else are only vanities that lead to nothing and are barriers to the Way. . . . All passions are evil, even those that lead to good. . . . Experience limited to knowledge is a sign of disease. . . . The wise man does not amass things. The more he gives, the more he gains. . . . Leave all things in order that all things may come."

All these diverse voices, coming from different horizons, merged together to contradict the dominant thought of the West, which invites us to knowledge, to power, to take, to possess.

I reread the Gospels as if I had just discovered them in a bookstall, not liturgically, without devotion, but just as I read Nietzsche. The Gospel gathers and condenses the wisdom of the Orient. There is the same call to inner upheaval, to awakening. At the same time it is a revelation, since it points to a love whose logical conclusion is the communion of sharing. But what most startled me was the obscure perception that this word was the response to a long-felt expectation. There existed outside of me a word that spoke within me, beneath the idle chatter I had been nourished with. Of course, ambiguity still existed. An observer—and I was the observer of myself—was able to perceive in this interior word only a reworking of old phrases, images of a peasant childhood, too quickly identified with a metaphysical claim. But in spite of everything the belief never left me that all people still in touch with their primordial roots had heard this word murmured within themselves. The expectation of the unknown could be heard through the cultural deposit which continued to call "God, God," even when it spoke of nothingness.

For a long time I battled against the religion of my mother in the name of a purer idea. A wonderful illusion. In reality I was secretly detached from all faith. Aesthetics had taken its place—at least I thought so for a while. Everything happens in its own time. In dying my mother taught me a lesson. She refused every word of assurance, every consolation of religion. Then I realized that it wasn't only in the novels of Bernanos that the servants of God die abandoned and apparently in revolt. The death of my mother allowed me to detach myself radically from the folklore of religion, which is useful and even necessary in certain conditions, and made me a wanderer. I left forever the world of villages for the desert of cities. I resolved to do nothing to mask the emptiness and to keep myself as far as possible away from the whole pious circus.

But the first words of my mother, her voice, her gestures and the swaying of her body had been too strong. Her word came from the beginning of time, and in the cursed and cherished city it caught up with me. No longer able to walk on paths underneath the trees or along running streams, I let images of forests and water rise from my own depths, and suddenly there was a murmur: "Jerusalem, Jerusalem, how many times have I wanted to gather together your sons like a hen gathers together its chickens." I felt a certainty, even though my mind saw obstacles and absurdities everywhere. Agnosticism and skepticism remained intact in me. Nevertheless something was drawing me, a confidence in the night, like a gladness of the flesh which was perhaps not only flesh.

## Long Ago and Yet Again

Here's what happened after a few years. I had not gone back to my native village since the death of my mother. I decided to spend a couple of days there. For me it was as devastated as a Palestinian village, but in a different way because it had been invaded by progress. The old paths had disappeared along with the trees. Much of the land had been abandoned to the wind. The animals were now lodged in immense metal sheds. The river stank. What did it matter? I rediscovered places and objects, the worn steps of our house. The names of our dogs came back to me. I heard my mother's voice and with an unspeakable joy saw her face. I shook hands with people. Old phrases came back to my lips, local jokes. Everything was still going on. The tissue of language was stronger than the stones. Although debased by radio and TV it at least conveyed the changing seasons, the everyday worries, death and hope. I was immersed.

I didn't know what was going to happen. After returning to the road, I climbed to the top of the hill from where the whole village beyond the cemetery can be seen at once. I took a last look and expelled it all forever. It now seems to me that if I've met so many wounded men and women, nomads and strays, who have contacted me because of my books in the illusion that I possessed some secret that was not in the text, it was because I had renounced all rootedness. (Nevertheless, when someone has lived his childhood and adolescence in a village, he carries it with him all his life.) However, I don't recommend this practice for anyone. When one survives, one is cleansed of many desires and fears. But there is a long and difficult moment to undergo, a face-to-face encounter with death. Surely it would be better to wait for *it* to take place.

## *Perhaps, in Spite of Everything, He Loves Me*

Just as the Gospel again beckons to me, something like this is said. God is unknowable. I don't know if he is loving. Nature bears witness to intelligence, certainly, but also to barbarism. He is as cruel as he's tender, as indifferent as attentive. It's advisable to break apart all those formulas we use to construct a god in our image. To say no to God out of fidelity to God is the approach of the Bible.

I don't know God. I am within—living in the emptiness hollowed out by my self-sufficiency. The fish doesn't know the water which makes it live, only the absence of water from which it dies.

I know God only through Jesus. The unique grandeur of Christianity is its belief in a poor God, like a wound in the absolute. God, the child in a manger. No man could invent that; it requires a revelation.

Jesus was not born at Jerusalem. Bethlehem, if it was Bethlehem, has nothing in common with the temple or with Greek temples, which are machines designed to exorcise the world of contingency, or with the temples of India, like Elephanta with its breathtaking stone Trimurti. God has the fragility of an unprotected child. Jesus supports us, he helps all wanderers, he is on the side of nomads. Heaven was his roof: "I never lived in a house."

To know something of his tenderness and his exactingness, it's enough to read the parables. Don't project them into history, but listen to them today, pronounced by the Spirit who is the spirit of Jesus. They are words that have to be fulfilled; otherwise they become pathetic legends to console us.

In years past we found irony in the fact that Jesus, the friend of the poor, the man of kindness and pardon, was betrayed, mocked, and assassinated. Today, for those whose faith isn't strong enough to bear the burden, the opposite is absurd. For example, it's seeing holy men, whom we salute in faith as representatives of Jesus, caught up in the games of history, still playing at being heads of state. It's seeing pious and worldly men, after proclaiming themselves disciples, angling for honors and meeting with almost universal approbation or indifference.

When I think of the tenderness of God, a page of Simone Weil comes to memory. This enigmatic Jesus, close to the one I discovered with amazement in rereading the Gospel, tells me more about the subject than any holy pictures or theology.

> He entered my room and said: "Poor creature, you who understand nothing, who know nothing. Come with me and I will teach you things which you do not suspect." I followed him.
>
> He took me into a church. It was new and ugly. He led me up to the altar and said: "Kneel down." I said: "I have not been baptized." He said: "Fall on your knees before this place, in love, as before the place where lies the truth." I obeyed.
>
> He brought me out and made me climb into a garret. Through the open window one could see the whole city spread out, some wooden scaffoldings, and the river on which boats were being unloaded. He bade me be seated.
>
> We were alone. He spoke. From time to time someone would enter, mingle in the conversation, then leave again.
>
> Winter had gone; spring had not yet come. The branches of the trees lay bare, without buds, in the cold air full of sunshine.
>
> The light of day would arise, shine forth in splendor, and fade away; then the moon and the stars would enter through the window. And then once more the dawn would come up.
>
> At times he would fall silent, take some bread from a cupboard, and we would share it. The bread really had the taste of bread. I have never found that taste again.
>
> He would pour out some wine for me, and some for himself—wine which tasted of the sun and of the soil upon which this city was built.
>
> At other times we would stretch ourselves out on the floor of the garret and sweet sleep would enfold me. Then I would wake and drink in the light of the sun.
>
> He had promised to teach me, but he did not teach me anything. We talked about all kinds of things, in a desultory way, as do old friends.
>
> One day he said to me: "Now go." I fell down before him, I clasped his knees, I implored him not to drive me away. But he threw me out on the stairs. I went down unconscious of anything, my heart as it were in shreds. I wandered along the streets. Then I realized that I had no idea where this house lay.
>
> I have never tried to find it again. I understood that he had come to me by mistake. My place is not in that garret. It can be anywhere—in a prison cell, in one of those middle-class drawing-rooms full of knick-

knacks and red plush, in the waiting room of a station—anywhere, except in that garret.

Sometimes I cannot help trying, fearfully and remorsefully, to repeat to myself a part of what he said to me. How am I to know if I remember rightly? He is not there to tell me.

I know well that he does not love me. How could he love me? And yet deep down within me something, a particle of myself, cannot help thinking, with fear and trembling, that perhaps, in spite of everything, he loves me.

There are some men and women who have a hobo in them, just below the surface. They are people whom a mere nothing can make happy, whether a blackbird on the grass, lichens on a wall, or a patch of sunlight on a tree. They live the instant completely. It's for them that I write.

## *A Meeting Always in the Future*

Nevertheless, the time has not come for me to try to represent Jesus personally. I'd like to avoid that word "represent." There are many obstacles to overcome. Certainly, from one point of view, the Gospel and Jesus are easy and immediate. Lightness and grace, by skimming above all knowledge, can create the intimacy that removes obstacles. On the other hand, our cultural distance from the New Testament is so great, the vocabulary that does our thinking for us is so anchored in our own time, the illusion that makes us rush to give what we find the name of what we are looking for is so insidious, that to truly encounter Jesus in an individual manner (and in this area every meeting can only be individual) a considerable effort, perhaps a battle, is necessary. You realize it only later. At first, if you haven't already fallen into boredom or disgust, you are led into religion by an instinct which makes you select certain things, perhaps with a bad conscience. For a lazy, docile conscience continues to dwell within us. A long time may pass while you struggle against clichés and sentimental bric-a-brac, always tempted to give up the whole mess and live precariously, unencumbered by any spirituality. But that's not easy either, because a word continues to stir in us.

Encounter—how I dislike that word! A meeting of that kind is never an accomplished fact, but always still to come.

Perhaps I'm simply reading the Gospel the way I read Nietzsche. Paradox and asceticism can be misappropriated and ultimately serve only to arouse fervor and enjoyment. Gide and Rilke excelled in that approach.

At the outset the fascination is much the same. Is the Gospel message only a mirror that reflects my own desires? I am somewhat asocial by nature because of my childhood, a stranger to the theater of the world, and I enjoy seeing power and pretense exposed. But do I have to suffer in order to understand; does an excess of *health* close the gates of the kingdom to me?

Nietzsche is not far from the central fire, but he needs lightning and thunder. He cultivates enthusiasm, frenzy and torture, hurls you into a whirlwind of light, and leaves you there, dazzled, immobile, and somewhat conceited. How can we escape the complacency of vertigo? Nietzsche is to be trusted only for his observation and analysis. By breaking words open and unveiling the mechanisms of attachment, he can bring us to rejection, but he may also leave us more open to what is coming.

Jesus, too, is disconcerting. He shatters our certainties, but not just to illuminate us; in the same instant he takes us along with him and proposes a communion.

One day I found myself at an international congress of theology, like a fish out of water. A Roman dignitary who liked my books had asked me to speak on "Christian language." During the discussion a well-known theologian declared, "What you say may be all right for you because you're an artist, but what becomes of the *content* of truth?"

"You're there to watch over that," I said in order to avoid a pointless argument.

But today my answer would be longer: "What have you classical theologians made of it? Weak soup for the dead. You've detached some abstract ideas from the text, accurate perhaps but dead because they are cut off from the body of the word. You have systematized them, transforming the message into a set of truths, and even if you haven't said so directly you've led people to believe that faith was simply a matter of accepting those truths."

Sooner or later, we must be liberated from that notion of faith. There is a healthy doubt that connives with authentic faith. The path of doubt frees us from faith in our own ideas, for we are apt to make an idol of truth, pliable to the laws of a cultural logic. But the truth, Pascal says, is not God.

For a long time I was paralyzed by the thought that perhaps I was adhering only to the surface of Christianity. A religious critic said it about one of my first books: "Everything takes place as if spirituality has been swallowed up by literature and aesthetics." I was tempted to maintain silence in regard to everything that directly concerned faith—thereby following the advice of a cardinal who told me,

"Speak of everything except religion if you want to stay out of trouble"—because I had been formed by such a shoddy theology and hadn't fully shaken it off.

Now I think I know a little better. Just as the sap in a tree can pass only through the bark, life is conveyed by a human word, not by disparate ideas. The word is *divine* (use a capital "W" if you prefer) not because of the idea but the breath. It sets everything in motion. It's certainly not up to me to decide what faith is. I put my confidence in it; my doubts are only in my head. My doubt and I are both in God. This hand that is writing knows better than I; it reaches out toward communion, even when it rejects false comradeship.

I want to situate myself prior to any formulation of faith, cry out in the desert, and point to the one who is coming.

## The Invisible in the Perceptible

Let's not be unfair—there's more than one theology. There are theologian-prophets today who liberate the Word, even if some of them think it's useful to express it in the conceptual categories of the atheistic philosophers of our time, as fascinated by them as others used to be by Plato and Aristotle. But conventional theology linked to specific intellectual positions is a gigantic hindrance to the reading of the Bible—that is, to the living body of the Word, and ultimately to faith.

Thinking that is indissolubly linked to Greek conceptualism, however brilliant in its origins, remains functional. This is because giving a name to the unknown means accepting the illusion that the one who names exercises a kind of control, neutralizing mystery by taming it. In spite of all declared intentions, its basic purpose is to control and to appropriate. That is the danger of such theologizing. It is linked with the mechanistic ideology of the West, which aims at power. All those dissertations on analogy are in themselves correct, but they don't change anything. Those people in the service of a religious ideology that is mistaken for faith participate in the assassination of Jesus. Of course, like everyone else, they know not what they do.

Such instrumental language is inevitably old and diseased, even when it borrows contemporary clothes and tries to be modern. Wishing to say too much too quickly, it no longer says anything. At the very moment it speaks of hope, something different is communicated: attachment, fear. Its partisans go on and on about "the contemporary religious crisis," but they always end up lapsing into nostalgia. If there is a crisis, it is because there is a *before* and an *after*, which relieves them of the responsibility of existing today. Whether looking back to a past, which they imagine as a golden age of faith, or projecting themselves into the future, they are prophets of illusion and dream—that is, of the artificial eternity of abstraction.

Haunted by an abstract pseudo-universalism their thought ignores the individual, the reality of the body and the present. The perceptible and visible become only passing illusions. In spite of their declared and sincere intentions, the flesh is denied, and hence the resurrection which becomes merely a mental certainty. Such a mode of affirmation opens up the way to negation.

The fundamental insight of the Bible, however, is that the invisible can speak only by means of the perceptible. There is no concept that will suffice for harvests turned golden, lilies of the field, the lost drachma, the wounded man on the road to Jericho. Similarly, only theology attempts to distinguish between faith, love and action, a distinction that has no foundation in Scripture.

A choice has to be made between ideology and the primacy of word/poem/action. The former is a doctrinal system that transforms what should be an interior birth into a categorical imperative: this is what you ought to think, believe, say. In this way the concrete human being is made subordinate to the idea, and we make someone a slave while telling her that she is free. By killing all creativity, one falls into sterile repetition, which produces both sadness and disaffection. I know what I'm talking about; I, too, played this game in all sincerity. Don't forget: I cooperated in this conditioning process after undergoing it myself.

It's not a question of rejecting reason. I am well aware of the fecundity of the "concept," which has made it possible for humans to dominate the earth. Without it we would have neither the sciences nor progress and modern conveniences. So what? We wouldn't have pollution or atom bombs either. But let's have a truce with hypocrisy: it's not a matter of either dreaming or scorning. We are part of the West; it would be childish to forget that fact. But let reason stay in its place. Some morning I'll try to explain why it seems to me that in the spiritual order it's appropriate to go beyond reason by means of reason.

## The Imaginary Absolute

For the moment I'm simply trying to recapture the thoughts that accompanied my rediscovery of Scripture. I had to wake up from the old human dream of the universal and absolute which I had confused with the love of God. For there is a time when you spontaneously identify hope with what is imaginary. You are driven by the need to free yourself from human limitations, so you say "God," "love." You use nostalgia as a cure for anguish. You thereby escape for a while into the euphoria of illusory fusions. There is a frenetic passion for the absolute, a taste for the marvelous and for miracles, that is only a camouflage for self-love, one means among others to bottle up desire by refusing to surrender the dream, face up to reality and set out on one's journey. It is possible to fall upon God as into vice.

Begin then by curing yourself of the desire to be God at any cost. Instead, return to your center, become one person among others in an experience based on brotherhood. In Christianity, unlike in Eastern religion, it is not the absence of desire that saves. Desire cuts through the event and becomes salvation when, by grace, it is transformed into oblivion and gift. Nevertheless, without denial or repression, one needs to be cured of desire in order to create space. For the God who fills human hunger is at the same time the Unknown, the Stranger. Only his absence-presence allows a person to be oneself.

To disappear is one of the deepest of human desires. It is the delight you experience on the borderland of sleep when you seem to just flow along, or the vertigo, when in love, of no longer being anyone, in any form of creation, in action, power or drugs. But to lose oneself spiritually it is first necessary to find oneself.

To be only what one is, to consent to the fragility of existence, to refuse to be everything and everywhere in illusory fashion by surrendering to the magic of abstraction, to stop making God the idol of a dream, to create a new relationship—this is the way. When people discover their own truth, there bursts forth an alleluia that permeates all that lives without putting obstacles in the way.

Every authentic spiritual life, it seems to me, first goes through disappointment. A day arrives when we hate illusions, and perhaps we then become less dishonest disciples, a little more capable of hearing the word.

Perhaps we don't really become adult until we have understood that everything is vital enchantment, as John Cowper Powys says— that is, illusion. It becomes as impossible to settle down in one place as it is to make motorcycling a permanent way of life. Spiritual life implies a constant sobering up in order to enter a greater joy. What is ultimate meaning if not this movement within us that runs through all our desires, the almost nothing which makes us live and kills us at the same time?

## A Word Recreated by Men and Women

I believed at first what they taught me, that *one* overall attitude could be extracted from the Gospel, a sort of synthesis, easy to handle. I believed that humility and obedience encouraged us to be satisfied with it; all that was needed was to hunt here and there for chapter and verse to illustrate it. Little by little I came to recognize something which many of those who taught me, held back by fear, were not unaware of. Research on the New Testament indicated that vital tensions were expressed within it. It seemed obvious that to reduce these differences would cut people off from the roots of faith.

We have only a clumsy and sometimes pathetic vocabulary with which to express the Gospel message. For a long time we naively believed that our languages would be able to uncover its ultimate meaning. Discoveries in anthropology, ethnology, and linguistics no longer permit us to think so.

Besides, we only know with certainty some of the words of Jesus. The others? On many occasions the Master gets impatient with his disciples who understand nothing. And Jesus didn't write, didn't dictate anything. But how are we to be certain that those who wrote things down and those who edited the texts haven't left out something essential? Faith doesn't mean credulity.

To venerate the Gospel as a sacred object which automatically produces beneficial effects is to practice magic. Genuine respect calls for constant research. Just as it was necessary for Jesus to go away in order for the Spirit to come, it is also necessary that his word be tossed out, nourished, spread abroad and recreated by men and women with the random influences of particular individuals, environments and circumstances. The important thing is not our believing in it but that "it should grow within us," as Claudel says. There is an inexhaustible richness in this fact. The difference in perspective among the Gospels, their lacunae, ambiguities or contradictions— even our uncertainty as to what belongs to Jesus and what is the product of copyists and scribes—enlarges the freedom of Christians. There can no longer be any question about it. Spiritual pluralism is inscribed in the texts themselves, as it was in the experience of the first disciples. Unity cannot be established from the outside by ideology; it is an interior reality and takes root within differences.

How many times I asked myself if I could be totally impersonal—simply obedient, adhering to the official Jesus which had been made obligatory. But the answer was always no, not without betrayal. The impersonality and forgetfulness that hide behind the veil of fidelity indicate abdication and laziness. What I want to hear is the Word cried out at constant risk just as Jesus offered himself to every risk. I want a word that is spacious, unprovincial, not the stilted language of devotion, not tiresome harping and academic commentary. Let preaching be the Gospel today. Let it be an encounter, having form and breath, with the text and interior word that speaks in every one of us, the same word, yet different. It's pointless to talk about the resurrection if *our* words have not been raised again, unless joy beats its wings within us.

## The Messiah Rescued from the Scribes

I am not asking everyone to invent his or her own Jesus but merely to understand how unforeseeable he was. Naturally, we always read the Gospel in terms of our own desires. When I speak of Jesus, whether I want to or not, I'm speaking about myself. One can realize this and still keep one's sense of humor.

My meaning should be clear. Unity can't be imposed from without. It's impossible to avoid risk or the need to interiorize one's faith. To answer me by denouncing subjectivism and fideism is simply to use dubious philosophical structures. We should replace philosophical pseudo-rigor with spiritual rigor. To wall God up within the distinction between subject and object is nothing but childishness. Every message that does not ripen in the individual conscience is dead. Through the individual to the universal.

Doctrinal unity, however necessary, is ultimately only an administrative unity. To tame the mystery by employing only one firm and unique meaning is a dream, a dream of power. Am I saying that everything should be allowed to crumble and dissolve? That would be to forget the Spirit who is the bond of unity. The Church has no need of power to sweep us along by its very size in the manner of political societies. Meaning organized according to some rational process that tries to substitute itself for the Word is a rejection of the Holy Spirit.

This is why the Messiah who has come is always still to come, to rise again, to be rescued from the scribes. An interpreter of the Gospel can only be an explorer and prophet, not the administrator of its meaning. For the word is, above all, linked to concrete life and events, not some system of thought. The word was never pronounced to overwhelm reason or to convince it, but to set us in motion. Its power precedes clarity. A summons, it cuts through contradictions without even taking notice of them.

No Gospel exists in its original freshness. Once the familiar grids in which we've been taught to read it are removed, it becomes very upsetting. At that point it's useful to look at the text more closely with the help of specialists whose role is to say, "Here are some possible meanings; feel free in regard to the inner sense." We have begun to understand how much separates us from the time and place of the Gospels, the distance between them and Jesus, and their divergent orientations. The essential task is this: to forget what we know or believe we know and to receive the text in its purity, to be brought alive by its breath. We undoubtedly need a kind of grace to recover our second innocence.

Besides, those grids of interpretation are never completely removed. We never find ourselves face-to-face with the Gospel itself. But that's fortunate. Otherwise, what would there be left to say?

To view the literal meaning of Scripture as an absolute is a roundabout way of rejecting the Word, which must be a new creation. It's seeing God behind us when in fact he is always ahead of us, unpredictable. A word that is completely divine, objectified, a form of knowledge, will only produce slaves; it would be the funeral monument Hegel speaks of.

And why should the Gospels be readily accepted? Breath, rhythm, gesture, parable and paradox—poems—are at once simple and secret, and can be only gradually unveiled. A poem accomplishes what it speaks of, but through a process that is never complete. The persons who receive it must return into darkness where they will never finish exploring it. The idea of exploiting it never occurs to them. Instead, they allow it to grow within them, to occupy more and more space. Bad poets do harm by trying to cash in on their talent; they think they possess it, since they're not at all possessed by it. The poem of the Gospel deals with existence and is intended to rise like yeast. Its style is just the opposite of a message that tries to control our lives with slogans and principles.

If Jesus is often rejected before being given a real hearing—or worse, if he is admired as a great man, a "hero of our civilization"— it's because piety has presented such a lukewarm, legalistic, sometimes even worldly, image; it is because the malleability of children and "the poor" has so long been exploited to fabricate worshipers, and because many are still discussing a dead man even when they think they're talking about resurrection.

## Insurrection and Resurrection

How was it possible?

How could the Gospels be poured out each Sunday as material for long speeches or self-justification? How could the poem have been so neutralized?

(When I say "poem," pay attention. The poetic, in the sense of picturesque or pretty, doesn't interest me. I am speaking of something indissolubly linked to the actions of life—gestures, a manner of existing, an ardor. It's impossible to remove the poetry without destroying the Gospel; it's part of it or it isn't. . . . )

Our indifference is part of the answer, along with a false idea of obedience, verbal bombast, boredom. But can we expect all university professors to be pioneers, all parish priests to be prophets, all bishops to be successors of the apostles? Each of them has been recruited haphazardly, with his own share of goodwill, insight and blindness, his own wounds and ambitions. I'm not shocked by this. I'm not preaching purity. Jesus is delivered up; he always will be. *It is necessary that these things happen.*

Ordinary people like us identify with the story of the child hunted by Herod, with the young man of thirty who was always on the go, whose own family considered him mad, with the one who was crucified and rose again, with that rebel whom every society—sometimes by using violence, sometimes veneration—will inevitably try to keep from spoiling everything. There is something amazing in the process of assimilation and neutralization that has been going on for many centuries. But what is even more amazing is that always, within the womb of illusion and hypocrisy, lost in the crowd, there have been saints. The word has never ceased finding its way into the flesh of men and women.

Our task is to live the benediction and the insurrection at the same time, the love and the humor, the unimportance of everything and its infinite importance. Sometimes I have the illusion that I am on the verge of learning how, which frightens me without my knowing why.

I've given up trying to enter into the heads of those who know how to sprinkle the Gospel with current ideologies. I can't do it; each word hurts. Having neither the courage nor the grace of the martyr, held back by my own mediocrity, all I have to offer is the written word with which I may be able to nourish a few rebels. They, too, are the faithful.

In any case, it's impossible not to see that at the heart of the Gospel there is a radical rejection of all convention. Its uniqueness does not lie in some idea that will harmonize all differences but in its tone: the shock which upsets our complacency and invites us to interior reappraisal.

Socrates' confidence in knowledge was total. He aimed to correct false judgments by means of a rigorous mental arithmetic. Such assurance doesn't exist for Jesus, who invites us to set out en route right away. I would be embarrassed to cite texts to prove all this. I'm tempted to give in to the scribe in me who wants to show his power. But there's nothing to prove. Just read Mark and the others. I am not teaching; I simply speak of what's inside me. I write for those who carry the Gospel within them, who know the Gospel or are getting to learn it by heart.

## A *Splinter in the Flesh of the World*

If one wants to distinguish, there are two layers in the Gospels. On one hand, there is a rejection of all conformism, an invitation to awareness communicated by a boldness of tone. On the other hand there is love and the community of sharing whose perceptible sign is bread and wine—the Eucharist—which is both death and resurrection.

If love is not to be reduced to a new formalism or community to ritual while pretending to overcome divisions of money, class and race, they have to avoid ideology and sentimentalism, which means that they must begin to be fulfilled. Otherwise, in spite of all good intentions, love and ritual become only more examples of inertia, made worse by fakery. To believe that love can be intellectualized and made as obligatory as ritual, that people can be taught about a community of sharing in abstract terms, is to open the way to all sorts of illusions.

Don't cut corners. The Gospel is not made to dominate the world. It's the grain of sand that upsets the world's machinery. One can't inhale its fragrance and be content to leave everything the way it is.

Despite recent superficial adjustments, Jesus is still crushed under the weight of ideological shackles and worldly-minded hierarchies, just as he was crushed under the cross. Emperors are no longer crowned or deposed in his name but in too many countries he remains the symbol of social and political immobility.

There is a danger in thinking about glorification.

Glorification always ends up in the system—in power. But Jesus' message is the opposite of power, turning respect and judgment upside down, as in the Magnificat.

The illusion was this: Because revelation ended in glory (which one believes in the obscurity of faith), glory was spread over the whole adventure before the right time had arrived, so we then tried to impose the order of glory in morality and politics. Despite denials, this illusion persists in many minds. Just as Jesus, insofar as we can imagine him in human terms, did not know everything and experienced genuine agony, we too can only live in the darkness of expectation, even though the darkness is luminous. There is always a danger in exploiting faith as a form of human *knowledge.*

There's no point in *proclaiming* an abstract certitude, whether the virginity of Mary or the resurrection of Jesus. They can only exist in us as an infinitely discreet light. *Truth waits for dawn in the gleam of a candle.* Proclamations are attempts to install ourselves in a rigid order of glory. But it's the poverty and pain that men and women undergo which contain the seeds of Jesus' glory.

Don't fool yourself. When the soldiers took off his clothes and covered him with a scarlet cloak before putting a crown of thorns on his head and a reed in his right hand, crying, "Hail, king of the Jews," they were enacting the ultimate truth of all time.

What is ridiculous is to see crowds come together and sing the Credo, some making claims in the name of the past, others in the name of the future, always with the same hunger for miracles. Jesus' whole effort is to lead each of us back to his or her center, where decisions are made.


## Only One Road, Mine and Yours

Savior, Messiah, Son of God, Risen One—these glorious titles veil the image of the Galilean, just as richly decorated copes and golden monstrances prevent us from seeing the tortured man or understanding the humility of bread and wine. There is a need for security among teachers who proclaim the official truth, and a corresponding need among those taught, which gets covered over by the name of *faith.* It would seem that for many believers it is essential for Jesus to be first of all *declared* God, Christ. They have it in their heads, tamed, fixed in formulas—formulas intended for everyone and for no one—which dispense them from ever realizing to what extent Jesus' concrete existence was that of a rebel. How can they be blamed? They have been manipulated, "broken" as we break in a horse.

It is boredom, fatigue, the horror of embalming, of voices too full of honey or bitterness, of abstract formulas repeated ad nauseam, and finally a certain sanity of mind that has left so many men and women unable to endure hearing us speak of the Lord, Christ, or divine liberation. The real human choice is the choice for or against money, or success at any cost, for or against love (which, far from being used up in what Pascal calls "the harnessing of concupiscence," unmasks it), for or against the uncontrolled pleasure that divides as against the joy that unites. In the spiritual order, when we want to say something, it's often better not to mention its name too often so that language doesn't become a substitute for living reality. Let it be transparent in a face, or the inflection of a voice. What is salvation or liberation if it is not born out of the experience of emptiness and abandonment and if it does not liberate anyone? Many people, it seems to me, do not explicitly reject the salvation of Easter and may be pursuing it their own way.

What is shocking is to make use of God's humility and discretion in order to control things by means of power.

One day the question forced itself upon me: How can one avoid the split between Jesus and Christ? On one hand, let's not make him a symbol, projecting either our nostalgia or our revolutionary aspirations on him. On the other hand, let's not borrow his authority to impose faith by blackmail.

Glory and salvation are not to be found except along this path. The peasant-rabbi is not born of philosophy or theology; he is the way. Therefore, it is by following him step-by-step in the humility of childhood, in the hidden life of his first thirty years, in his battle against and with the law, against the scribes, Sadducees, and Pharisees, in the distance he kept from his family, in his fidelity to the Father, that he is the Liberator. To claim to believe in him without going through a metanoia, upsetting our old chain of values, is simply a farce. Glory is to be found in humiliation.

Don't insist that he be adored. Don't even try to make anyone believe. That will happen, or it won't, depending on individual maturity and grace, in a living experience of salvation like that of the first Christian communities. Abrupt affirmations are never revelatory when life says nothing, offers no invitation. The word is adaptable only in oneself, in the empty play of thoughts that are often potent seeds.

It's impossible, therefore, to short-circuit questions with prefabricated answers. Following him is all that counts. There is only one way, mine, yours—a way lit up by the Gospel and the Church which is the servant of the Gospel.

Let the Church have faith in God, Jesus Christ. Let it become transparent. That's enough. Let it live by that faith. The news will get around.

Don't jump to the conclusion that I scorn everything that exists. Dreams of spotless purity come cheap. I'm not setting up dream against reality. Reality is more beautiful than any dream, once we rid it of the illusions that we mistake for it. In the Christian community, liberated at least interiorly from its historical attachments, divested of its finery, and centered on humanity on the march, there is space, freedom, discovery and laughter for anyone who wants it and who has nothing to lose or gain. I inhabit the Church *created by the Word*, born and always to be born, the Church of Mark, Luke, Matthew. I admire Paul and I put up with him, including the unfortunate degree to which theologians have been able to conceptualize and systematize his fanatic lyricism. With John I battle against Paul, against the law and ritualism which he surreptitiously reintroduced. I leave that Church only in order to be present in another manner. Futurologists and traditionalists, partisans of every kind, those who never speak, charismatics who want miracles in order to escape the rough, humble path of ordinary people—all are strangers to me. Nevertheless, everywhere, under all those shriveled forms, in all the ideological splits, there are disciples. I feel in solidarity with them all, across our differences, as well as with those who no longer want to hear about God or Jesus.

I write in order to breathe, to enlarge my space, to meet brothers and sisters, to practice a new kind of freedom.

## To Read Is To Emigrate

Human beings are not looking for just anything but for the absolute, even when they believe they are turning away from it, or when they unknowingly repress it in a search for material things. Every passion is an arrow aimed at the other shore. Literature speaks of the passionate experience of those purified in the fire of consciousness and risen from death. It is an interior demand, a movement of the body, emerging from the hand more than the head. Ideas, even when they are about the future and eternity, speak only of death. Literature—at least when it tries to avoid complacency—is able to capture everything that rises. The only kind of writing that interests me is one that opens up on the impossible and the unknown. Such is my way.

It is only one way. According to it, to read, as well as to write, is to emigrate.

School and society as a whole fail to teach us how to read. They teach us to hold on and grab. Reading is completely pointless if it doesn't teach us to understand life, especially the burning passion of life itself. Of course, in order to read it is necessary to have roots, to experience in oneself the earth's heartbeat, but to read is also to reach out. Books that answer the need for nostalgia or merely offer knowledge can be read only with the intention of staying put. The Gospel, however, plunges us into the openness of the instant. It is the book of rebellion. To read it is to be born elsewhere.

Sometimes the word is indirect. It speaks of what is on the edges of reality in order to make those who listen aware of themselves. What is deep within us is beyond speech and can sustain itself only in obscurity, linked to an image, to the idea in its original state of excitement. Besides, to speak of what's deep down as against what's external no longer has meaning. The Word puts us in a state of grace, receptive to a discovery that will be unique each time, never definitive. It is always beginning.

It's hardly surprising that people prefer abstract formulas that can be repeated, clear but bloodless. Every reading of that type, regardless of what is meant, simply tends to legitimate and confirm the status quo, whether it invokes the fraternity of the first Christian communities or promotes progress.

The Gospels are bought, recited, commented on, quoted. They are not read any more than Balzac or Shakespeare, whose handsome bindings lend distinction to society drawing rooms. When they are read, it is through preexisting frameworks of interpretation, invoking ideologies that demand change only in order to stay the same. Why be surprised? Attitudes are made up of ideas, opinions and prejudices which form a protective shell. A new thought is accepted only when it has force on its side—that is, strength of numbers, when it becomes *normal* and can take its place in the overall system without danger.

But a spiritual message cannot possess the power of what is *nor-*

*mal* except by denying itself. So it must use the weapons of the rebel. The warrior of the spirit, who knows that meaning is always in a state of suspense, expresses himself through paradox, humor and parable. When, through fear of solitude or because of a flabby notion of charity, he comes to adopt the language of the tribe—a language which inevitably aims at permanence—his betrayal is greatest at the moment he is most applauded. If he refuses to take the broad and illusory path of "communication" it is because our everyday wisdom, with its lazy language of adaptation, offends him. He pierces our sleepy consciences and becomes in turn ironic, enigmatic, a killjoy. People start calling him paradoxical, destructive, or even crazy. If he's actually preaching the Gospel, they'll say he isn't familiar with the data. He ought to fit the text into the broader context. After all, it was written in another age. It would be dangerous if people started to realize that paradox simply unveils the hidden and crucifying reality within us, that truth is shy, that the path it opens up is endless, that harmony and calm exist only within the limits of everyday banality.

"He who knows how to tie has no need of cords," the Tao says, "and no one would know how to undo the knot." And Jesus asserts: "Give away also your robe. . . . Love your enemies." For the enemy is also part of us. It's necessary to get to the point at which I lose my identity in order to find it again in a different form. It's a kind of stripping, a harsh joy, which is why the Gospels aren't read.

The warrior of the spirit is never perfectly adjusted to society. He is like an exile. Don't fool yourself; he too wants happiness but in another space. Meanwhile, if he is happy, it's the happiness of the wanderer.


## Not for Sheep

In the last analysis it is the Gospel that inspires and guides the Church. Popes, bishops and priests are servants of the Word and our servants. They exist only to make sure it remains alive, and to point out the way to go.

If to read is to set out, to be transplanted, to create anew, we can see why the men of the Church find it so painful to read. After all, the way things are done now, it's as if they were the authors of the text. How can Christian communities be freed by the Word when they transform it into a form of knowledge to which they hold the key? The Church continually represses the prophetic voice until an event takes place that shakes it to its roots and unleashes the tide of the Spirit.

The Church may rightly reject heresy and be wise in doing so in terms of the laws of doctrine, but if it is guided only by abstract thought it will find itself situated outside life—that is, in heresy.

That is why we get restatements of doctrine, laments about "spiritual crises," barriers intended to slow things down but which simultaneously stifle the seeds of possible growth, and disciplinary interventions that repress both errors and appeals to new life. It's all done to protect the unchangeable character of faith in the belief that it's enough to declare one or another formulation true or false. However only the spiritual experience of men and women, as crystallized in a creative word, can provide light and warmth, thereby rendering "error" insignificant.

In the spiritual order an abstract affirmation satisfies only the person who makes it. It falsifies our progress along the way and degrades the poem of faith. Such people take a little girl and tell her, "Jesus is the Son of God; he has risen. You have to believe this as well as other things." Faith then becomes something ideal, a sort of artificial satellite of the mind that we can never catch up with, and end up by rejecting, or which we accept with a kind of dualism. This faith is an illness from which we must recover. Jesus the miracle-worker is the center of all our stories. We love God and others in a sublime interior space, which is simply a way of hiding and is ultimately a form of self-love inside the magic circle of an established vocabulary. In this way an ardent, intolerant faith often co-exists with sterile lives, and with no sense of fraternity.

Have you never run into any of those solid, sincere believers who constantly want to know whether you believe in the immaculate conception, or that the Son of Man is God, or that he rose again twenty centuries ago? If they could only realize that it is their unbelief that is speaking! How can they be brought to understand that some affirmations can kill—that the Gospel is linked to gestures, glances, and breathing, that it was made to be offered, eaten, and to become ourselves, reinvented, replayed, to merge with our silence as much as with our voices?

Jesus speaks of himself allusively and progressively. His disciples understand only much later, when they understand at all. No one has ever finished understanding. Don't have too much confidence, therefore, in those who say, "He is here, he is there." He is always elsewhere. To put forward a framed and final image does nothing but transform Jesus into an object of devotion or theme of reflection—which is precisely to make use of him to protect oneself.

To forget what one knows or believes that one knows, to participate in the kenosis, in the humiliation of God—that is the only way possible.

Jesus is present when he is not mentioned. He has many disciples beyond recognized frontiers who, if they are enemies of Christian salvation, are haunted by an abandonment that one might well call a kind of faith. The tactlessness of dualist affirmations has wounded them so deeply that one imagines they have had a spiritual experience. A taste for the absolute may have been communicated to them in their youth, but the only response to it that they learned was a doctrinal system. One day all that was left was erosion and emptiness. But in "the loss of their faith" they learned again the contingency of love seen in a face or in the misery of a child. Illusions, of course, are always possible; certain truths, when separated from their roots, run wild. But the ultimate meaning of Christianity is not in a world of ideas. It is a risk freely accepted when weakness and humility call out to us.

I do not *know*. No, I don't *know* if Jesus is the Son of God. I'm completely ignorant of the meaning of those words. My mental certainty is unimportant if my eyes, my gestures, my steps do not confirm it. And if Jesus is risen, it is at this very instant, in my relation to my neighbor—who is everyone, including my enemy. Every faith which doesn't speak out against prejudice and the barriers of race and class is nothing but an ideological and sentimental luxury.

I am saying a very simple thing which is scandalous only for those who are blind. If you possess faith as a mental object, if you're tense over it, disturbed, almost sick about it, if you have "problems" with it, then lose it and lose yourself. Perhaps faith will then be able to find you and take hold of you. If there was one thing in my limited experience that was electrifying, it was this: Several of the people who first most impressed me became rigid in what they called their "faith." It became a neurotic attachment to a system, a culture, a past, or a certain idea of the future.

A painful moment comes. You listen to eminent believers, people that you admire, even love. Suddenly you read something different in their words which gradually belies everything they're saying. At first it's a kind of liberation: you're through with the whole business. But it's not so simple. At a later time you again admire and grow close to these people. No one can ever express the totality of faith.

You yourself, who are so proud of your own approach, will be rejected in turn. It's better that way.

On the other hand, you may hear an agnostic or an atheist give a talk and with amazement you hear almost what Jesus would say. It's not external images that unite or separate people but something more secret and invisible.

I'm not saying what one must think, even if in spite of myself I take on a lordly air. I write because I'm fed up with ideology, with inflated forms of faith. I'm not writing for choir boys or for sheep. Those who write for sheep are bad disciples. I'd be ashamed to keep quiet. I'll arrive at the gates of paradise with my rejections and my doubts and will cry out with the leper, "I believe in you, Jesus of Nazareth." I believe unconditionally, Son of God or not, whatever we think those words mean. I believe he's risen, whether or not in the manner the resurrection was described in the past. I've always desired with my body that it was all true, even when my head was skeptical.

I'm exposing myself of course, not without some shame, in both meanings of the word. I'm exposing myself and also running some risks. But this path isn't mine alone. Perhaps others will be encouraged to come forward freely and independently. Sometimes I have the insane hope that because of these words, which hardly belong to me, a face will appear before which the angels hide their faces.

## The Way It Was

To find myself for a whole summer as a visitor on the edge of a town in upper Corrèze was to live again in a childhood locale, very near yet radically foreign to me.

Miraculously, a few traditional crafts survive. There is both a carpenter and a basket maker. And all around, everything is green.

At the end of the week some young people in helmets arrive from the city to blow off steam. They create a furor on the square among the gypsies who run the merry-go-round and sell holy pictures of TV stars.

It's better to rent a place than to be an owner—you're more free. Birds nest in the fake loft under the roof. At night you hear cries, chirping, a commotion followed by silence. The chirping starts up again and the noise is a relief. A lizard, a toad, a beetle, three shiny worms and two bullfinches live with us in the yard and along the hedgerow. Each night the toad stands guard by the door. We hear his unique note, pure and humble. All day and night there are seven sheep in the field nearby; we can hear them sucking the grass that has been pulled up and crunched. At dawn there are blackbirds among the sheep, a civet-cat pushes its snout through the hedge, in the woods nearby there is a hooting of a screech-owl, and here's a cuckoo. In the stillness of noon, pods of broom burst out like crackling flames. There is a sense of being immersed, of becoming part of something.

This is my home village with its farms scattered in the old manner, its paths, its banks, the babbling of tiny streams flowing through the grass, and trees everywhere, pillars of water rising to the sky.

Everything is green. I think of Galilee.

It's like a Breton village, pre-World War II, but without religion. Not one man at Mass, just a few elderly women. In my time social pressure encouraged attendance. I remember a parish mission. A Capuchin tried to get us to pray for a lost sheep who happened to be the bar-owner. I was on his side; I even brought it up in confession. Here the Mass takes twenty-five minutes ("What you are going to do, do quickly") including a ten-minute sermon which the priest has cribbed from some right-wing newsletter. The sermon is against money (this is a poor parish), against drugs (a problem unknown here), against divorce and eroticism (poor pious women!). It would have been good to hear a word that came from the depths. His back to the people, the priest goes on with his business but finds time to get us to recite three Our Fathers and three Hail Marys. We can hear the carousel on the village square. The voices of pop-singers fill the church, crying that love is all we need.

Bernanos would have been shocked by all this because he believed that hatred for priests showed a metaphysical vacuum. Here the priest is simply a piece of folklore. He operates a deserted service station and no one comes to see him. This does not prevent women who no longer go to church from bringing him some eggs, a chicken, or some country butter, largely because their grandmothers had done the same years ago. The men in the village generally salute him because he was a commandant during the Resistance. Hatred for priests exists only during the last stage of Christendom when the ecclesiastical bureaucracy tries to prolong its control artificially. Only tranquil indifference remains after power has been swept away, power which had once been offered as an image of the kingdom. The seeds of the Gospel are still invisible. Religious pressure, which considered itself above politics, has been replaced by another form of pressure which in the final analysis is probably less human. A new secular social order is in charge here, honest perhaps, but sad. Ordinary retired folk, the poor and the elderly, who hide out in rundown or pretty houses, are helped but kept apart. In India, Africa, or South America there is fraternity among the destitute, confidence in their eyes, and often something like joy. In our villages today and in our cities, the loneliness is overwhelming. Religious alienation has been replaced by the alienation of progress, the old consolations by TV. We are the third world of spirituality.


All around, everything is green.

I can't get Galilee out of my head. To think he remained silent for thirty years! Such a silence.

What was it like?

Did you find it natural? Were you able to go to sleep every night? Did you ever get angry? What part of you protested, which part was glad? Did you ever regret not being like others? Were you already moving away from your friends because of the emptiness in their eyes, which made solitude worse?

Was it necessary to hold God back?

As you walked in the upper part of the village where the sick and the elderly congregated in the evening light, did an old woman suddenly straighten as you passed? She's the one who walks with her head bent down to her knees and has an orange rooster with a fawn crest tied by a string to her door.

Did you have a special path to walk on, as we did, where you encountered a beetle here, a toad there, and two cottontails you recognize because they dwell in the innocence of another time? Was there a bush under whose shade you dozed—if you ever dozed—next to some dog or young donkey, and did the branches of the almond tree blossom out of season?

Were you obliged to be careful about the enthusiasm that flowed from you so you wouldn't overly upset the order of things? Did you have to hold God back or were you tempted to let miracles slip out of you in order to make up for things, just as words escape from us? It's forbidden. Your mission is to turn us back toward our center so we can find strength and love in ourselves. You're not supposed to pretend for us in order to disguise what has to take place.

Maybe initially you were without a past or future, existing totally in the openness of an instant-eternity, until the Word was uttered that shattered harmony and set you on the march.

Does God mature then?

He matured so much so that when, in your travels you found yourself in a village among your own people, they rushed out to take hold

34

of you, believing you crazy. The prudent Luke writes that "they took him to the brow of the hill . . . intending to throw him off the cliff."

So much for sentimentality.

## Why We're Impatient

As soon as mother had been finally put under the earth in her Sunday best, I tried to write a book of consolation and awakening. *Devance tout adieu* had some success, but after a few years I realized that nostalgia had led me to write a poetic exorcism.

My mistake was in portraying my mother while separating her from her world. I should have spoken about the villages, the slavery of women, the brutishness of men, injustice. Mother knew the Gospel by heart, but she had been indoctrinated by custom and the powers-that-be. She found the humiliated condition of women natural. Every original thought expressed in unconventional language delighted her at first but then seemed out of place. If some impulse prompted images and words that were sharp, she would blush at having let herself go. She undoubtedly accused herself of it in confession. There was only one humdrum road for her that led to salvation, and it concerned only the hereafter. All questions had their answers as shallow as the questions. People were so attached to formulas justifying submission and pain that the formulas had become sacred.

I've probably been unfair to the contemporary world where the terrifying passivity of populations is exploited by the audio-visual media. But this world already existed, approved, even blessed, by religion, with its catechetical slogans and functional morality. The benevolent backward glance one gives to an age past is never anything but disguised self-pity.

The only people who escaped this closed universe were madmen, some political agitators—who were obviously doing the work of Satan—and drunkards. Many others, after outbursts of anger, locked themselves into silence.

Hers was a system of social pressure justified by pious ideology, which neutralized criticism while permitting the wealthy to further enrich themselves and the powerful to rule. Because of it, my mother was never able to connect the Gospel that lived within her and her social existence. The message of liberation gave her neither assurance nor pride, and was ultimately only an inner melody distinct from the conventional language that did her thinking and directed her life.

35

Creation cannot be achieved, joy cannot exist, unless we resist the mechanism of language, its repetitions, its almost indiscernible terror. Neither intention nor attention is enough if we want to escape the vicious circle and reach self-truth. First, a kind of poverty is needed. Sometimes grace comes along afterwards.

Thinking doesn't mean recognizing or verifying what one knows but having a hunch, making a discovery—something quite distinct from having studious habits. As long as we base everything on closed intelligence, starting with inherited words that are not our own, we may believe we are masters of our thinking when in fact it is inhabited by death. However if we consent to be what we are and descend to the immemorial common basis of reality, we will happily discover that we are being guided.

As she lay dying my mother's faith, as regards its human supports, formulations, and religious objects, suddenly crumbled. This good woman lived through an agony of abandonment. I experienced it with her, insofar as such words can mean anything. Pride was already mingled with her pain. Pride in what? That she had crossed the line before dying, as far as I could judge, and had understood something, although I couldn't say what.

Certainly I was following my nature by choosing to live far away from the "glory" that the world reserves for those who glorify it. Nevertheless, it sometimes seems to me that my "mission" (using the word with gentle irony) was to read the Gospel she had passed on to me in her own way.

I now understand better that in order to do that I had to create some distance, to make myself a wanderer so I could offer that Gospel to others as a message of freedom in a collectivized world. Our world is prepared for every form of slavery and is more ruthless beneath its surface liberalism than the one in which my mother lived.

Against all reason I was led to speak about the sovereignty of the *individual*—I used that word on purpose—and to say that no society, however just and free, could be human if each person did not have his or her own space. One needs space in order to have access to one's own spirit—not as a shelter, but as a springboard. I also insisted that today and the present moment are more important than any projects or plans.

Readers who wrote to praise me—and I was delighted by their compliments—ended up by alerting me. They were nursing their nostalgia along with mine. My book was like a mirror for them. I had to tear myself away from that comfortable and sterile game and follow a different route than that used by most writers, especially those Christian writers who never managed to stop going around in circles and who developed a clientele among the living dead. There was no merit in that. I couldn't do it. I no longer knew how.

It was then that I began to understand better why. In what people called my novels, the leading roles went to people who had been wounded by life. Rejected by the world, they bore obscurely within themselves societies that were yet to be born. Without knowing or wishing it, they spontaneously isolated themselves from mind-sets and structures that sacrificed individuals to growth, money, the future, or to the image of happiness coming from the outside and that was even more alienating than the eternal happiness of cemeteries which have lulled so many believers to sleep.

For more than forty years I had repressed the voice that lived within me. Not only did I not dare rebel, I did not even entertain the idea of rebelling. I satisfied myself with nibbling outside the enclosures because I believed strongly in the necessity and durability of order. Until I came into contact with young people, with those who remained young even at an advanced age, and with a few of the poor, I couldn't understand and wouldn't take a chance. It's only recently that I've really begun to write. That's why I'm impatient at my age. No, that's ridiculous—I will never be my age. I'll be dead before that happens, so you've got nothing to worry about. Let me go on raving in my corner. Your orders will always be powerful, but, thank God, there will always be rebels prepared to hurt you and to cure you with their shameless joy.


## Lighthearted, They Walk in Darkness

First morning of autumn. Seems like spring. Impossible to write. But I have to get back to the Jesus of my reading. I went out to walk near the ponds of Ville-d'Avray. Such a gleam of light above the water-lilies; it's a morning to set out for somewhere. I constantly need to remind myself to slow down. To approach the subject, to suggest a beginning is all I can do for the moment, and pray that something happens. Faces emerge along the paths near the water, faces of friends, living and dead, who accompany me under the morning trees for part of the way.

I'd like first to speak of a certain kind of people. They aren't good at judging others. They respect differences but are implacable in uncovering intrigue. Their lips are trained to hear words that are not pronounced.

They're skeptics, supported by a "faith" that exposes the futility of opinions and beliefs, while remaining intransigent on the essential. But they are lovers of life, lighthearted, perhaps especially because they walk in darkness. Strangers to prestige, their lives are an insult to every power, although they bow to princes. They don't have much taste for obedience, and even less for giving orders. Their sense of the ridiculous holds them back.

Nevertheless, the men and women I speak of do their work as well as any, and without frenzy. Look at them carefully. In the depth of their eyes you'll notice an ironic gleam, an awareness of death.

Such people have little patience for calculations, regrets, remorse. We're already pardoned. The past does not exist. For them moral agonizing is an illusion based on attachment. Everything starts this instant, a new beginning. Hence there is no need to acquire or hoard, to construct a rampart, to find an excuse for being important outside of oneself. But the joy to create, yes.

To convey a sense of exuberance, of spending instead of hoarding, to encourage the role of foolishness, to break away for a while—such is their mission, unchosen, which has come to them in spite of themselves.

Their intention is not to disparage or scorn or destroy, but to arouse an interior movement that clears away waste and plows a straight line, so that the soul will rise up, prepared for new seasons.

Don't mistake them for fanatics of anti-fanaticism. Yet, being almost alone and against everyone, how can they avoid becoming unjust in order to resist mediocrity? It's easy for you to point out their intolerance, but their excesses are due as much to your cowardice and pretense as to their wild dreams.

Covered with scars, survivors of battles to which they rarely refer, they realize that they've been given a stay of execution. It feeds their sense of humor.

Certain words bring smiles to their eyes: happiness, progress, humanity, God. They indulge in no proselytizing or propaganda. They leave evil to itself. They let good inhabit them, since they value it so much.

Our many-faced contemporaries and TV smooth-talkers fill them with horror. They're anxious, therefore, to listen to those who speak with their own voice—or at least try to—and to make themselves heard, but not just by anyone, anywhere. The word has need of a space.

Delighted in turn by forests and city lights. Close to the grass, or to a passing dog. Physically happy with almost nothing. Naive? Don't believe it. They're neither good nor guilty nor innocent, capable of wounding as well as healing. Sometimes virulent, radioactive, exactly the opposite of what's at the basis of official doctrine—defining principles and saying, "Submit and you'll be free."

People without laws, they carry their own laws within them, unwritten, more demanding than your codes. They sense instinctively the element of hatred in organized charity and they know how to decipher the unfathomable sadness on the faces of our sentinels of duty. Hence their taste for pleasure, especially for the joy to which the sobriety of pleasure can lead. They know that without denial pleasure is degraded and that joy is never the product of self-gratification.

They come from far away. They have thousands of years on their side, and history does not speak of them. So what? Institutions endure with their own puppets, heroes and martyrs, but so do these others, and they are invincible. They have friends to laugh with. When they're dying, they wink at you just for a second, but it stays with you for life.

What do they have to do with Jesus? I don't know.

They don't take the trouble to watch processions go by. They don't climb up the sycamore tree. But since they're naturally attuned to paradox and parable, they are capable of attention and openness. Don't assume that they allow themselves to be fooled by words like faith, salvation, Christ, or love, which so many have bandied about. It's been too long since hearts skipped a beat underneath those surfaces. But the tone of a voice, a special gesture, a look. Perhaps a meal taken in common, a gesture with meaning.

## Are You Going To Laugh?

Nevertheless, don't expect Jesus to support my ideas, opinions or morality. He is the unknown who flushes us out from every cover, dodges our questions and makes us set out alone. His language consists of acts, parables and paradoxes, not ideas, because ideas are too impressive and attract followers.

It ought to be possible to reconcile the Jesus we know in the text—yet who is immeasurably distant from the text—with the Jesus whose breath was as unique as the situations, sins and scars of real existence. It ought to be possible, but it's never fully done, just as each communicant takes a morsel of the Eucharist yet receives it entirely.

How do you speak of the easy confidence felt on a road trodden by many others, and at the same time have a clear awareness that it's hardly a road at all, just a village footpath like those we made through the brush on the way to Mass? Important people who arrived by carriage never used it.

Instead of satisfying our desires, Jesus sends us back to ourselves at a deeper level. Morality, politics, economics, the intellectual harmony I keep looking for—none of these are his concern. He points in another direction; he drives me toward nothingness.

Don't campaign, therefore, for some fixed idea about Jesus. Otherwise you make him an idol: Jesus assassinated by his own kind. Because Jesus doesn't have a vision. Aristotle has, and Plato (after betraying Socrates). Aquinas has one, and Teilhard. But Jesus offers no plan except to go on to his death. He lives in another time-frame. One might say that his only desire is to tear us away from the known and marry us to another time, making death a path to life, after which everything—morality, politics, economics—takes a new direction toward something both impossible and necessary.

Stripped bare, disconnected, I lose all importance: my fortune, my name, my age, my race—the whole works. Like him whose tomb is empty. He is going away, but going not in order to have us become attached to images and phrases. Nourished by the bread and wine of his Word, our actions communicate him in the cup of cold water we give to the poor. When he is projected into history or enclosed within the logic of short-term purposes, he becomes a chief or a hero, a god made to our own small proportions.

When abstract ideas take over, real communion becomes impossible, through the very process by which they impose conviction: they try to fix reality, taking up position in an effort to keep watch. Past and future become the center of interest, not the present; the arrangement and balancing of ideas become central, not life itself. But tomorrow will take care of itself. Leave the dead alone. Wake up from your sleep. Rise, and come forward.

Or let knowledge become a dance. Dance follows laws but leaves no fixed trace. It destroys as it creates and thus completes itself in a new creation, an ever-new song.

Are you going to laugh?

I don't like people who love Jesus and talk about it. Yet here I am, talking about him. How do they know they're not simply in love with the image of Jesus that they have created? And what about me?

I can understand the vocabulary problem. But how can you say, without laughing, that you've met him? You'd stop drawing a salary, you'd be pointed out in a crowd, you'd be crucified. Someone who claimed to have seen him and ran away and continued to pile up money and glory—that I can understand; I'd be ashamed to require others to be holy while I drag myself along in mediocrity. But what should we think of those who encounter Jesus, speak with a quaver in their voice, yet continue to stuff themselves at the trough?

Some people experience new happiness, serenity of spirit, and murmur "God" and "love." Spiritual eroticism can take many forms. Then one day they suffer some interior hurt; God disappears, and they "lose" their faith so as not to admit it never possessed them. Words are fragile bridges. We have been too well taught to say "I believe," "I love." We naively decide that we've arrived, that our plan has been achieved, when we've scarcely begun the journey.

People I've met who were truly inhabited by faith were generally silent about the essentials and spoke of other things. They can only love what he loved: curing the sick, raising the dead, using words when there was nothing better, being hungry for justice, looking at things differently, reversing the spiritual order of this world.

Yes, I'm tired of hearing that Jesus is this or that. Even if we have no sense of shame, you'd think prudence would make us respond as his disciples did when Jesus enjoined them to say nothing. Instead of making him an easy object to manipulate, his unknown, untamed side should be left submerged.

To be unable to read or hear the Gospel without a shiver, beyond feeling and thought, on the verge of weeping; to know that this condemns you in the eyes of the enlightened; then, after spending a good part of our life resisting folly, pretending to be reasonable; wanting a foretaste of sanctity, praying for it, in order to be able to speak loud and clear. But in that case we would be silent. For how can we dare to proclaim words which are fulfilled only in our imagination or in rituals performed within a cultural circle and when we haven't extricated ourselves from lies? How can we transmit the Gospel if we only have the courage of a rabbit?

Mark is astonishing because he makes his discoveries gradually and is filled with wonder at everything. I like the fact that he doesn't seem to know where he's going. His problem hasn't been solved, and it won't be before the end of time. In his Gospel everything is about looking and listening. If he looks and listens through other eyes, other ears, what difference does it make?

A sense of wonder dominates the text of Mark. Astonishing, unpredictable—that's how the Galilean appears. "I haven't come for the just" (2:17). Surrounded by a packed crowd, he boards a small boat and speaks from the water to the people along the shore (4:1–2). One day with the disciples on the lake he says, "Let's cross to the other side." A storm comes up; he lies sleeping in the stern, resting on the shipowner's pillow (4:35–38). A young girl is dying; he speaks to her and she gets up. In the hubbub that follows he's the only one who realizes that she might be hungry (5:35). Don't speak of this to anyone. Near Tyre he enters a house but doesn't want it known (7:24). Why this obsession with silence and secrecy, since he himself says, "There is no secret which will not be revealed, nothing hidden which will not be brought to light" (4:23)? He disappears in the middle of the night; they look for him and find him alone in prayer. They bring his mother to him, and he asks, "Who is my mother?" (3:33). Even more than his words, his actions are inexhaustible parables.

They go across wheatfields and Jesus says that the sabbath was made for man, not man for the sabbath. Why does he eat with tax collectors and sinners? A blind man who has just been cured begins to see people as walking trees, so Jesus intervenes again. They bring him a paralytic, lowering the patient through the roof, and Jesus says, "Your sins are forgiven" as if all sickness came from sin. A possessed man calls him Son of God and two thousand pigs hurl themselves from a cliff into the sea. Fear becomes stronger than amazement; the people ask Jesus to leave.

He captivates crowds, but not in the manner of political leaders who need crowds in order to exist. He says astounding things, performs cures, slips away. One would think that he dreads miracles and simultaneously wants to show himself and to hide. He has a powerful understanding of propaganda but ultimately uses it to bring individuals to act for themselves. Imagine a public relations genius who successfully launches a product and suddenly declares, "Watch out: you're being fooled. It has nothing to do with miracles—it's something else." Or better, imagine a powerful political leader who breaks the illusion, stops using his talent for deception, reverses the supposed order of priorities, and talks directly to the men and women of today. He'd be shouted down, eliminated.

A mob, to the degree that it is a mob, can't hear a spiritual message. When a crowd (a large number gathered in one spot) or the public (a large number spread out over a wide area) gets excited, it's never on behalf of truth. Truth is used as a pretext. A crowd is governed by physical laws. To love the crowd—that is, the individuals who make up the crowd—means first keeping some distance from it.

Jesus seems to dread superficial commitment because he knows what it's made of. His message is not addressed to the crowd but to each individual in the crowd. He first breaks the connections, interrupts the conditioning process. Terms like "mankind," "humanity" and "crowd" aren't in his vocabulary; they're concepts. It's ideology and politics that take possession of the crowd as crowd—that's their function. To flatter the crowd, to love it while pursuing one's own ends, is contempt masquerading as love. If Jesus took hold of a crowd, it was in order to wrench free men and women from it, to look at them face-to-face. He wants them to pass from alienation and sleep to an awakening that makes genuine commitment possible.

Mark sees him turn back to the crowd and confront it, shattering sentimental illusions. The same thing happens in John 6 in front of a mob hungry for miracles which goes away discouraged by his incomprehensible words. To disappear, to rub people the wrong way, is typical of the Nazarene. If any want to follow me, he says, let them deny themselves and take up their cross. What's the point of gaining the whole world if one loses one's life?

Jesus: a man who causes divisions. He travels overnight into pagan territory after arguing about Jewish observances (7:24).

There's a danger in our understanding too quickly. Parable and paradox keep the message at a distance, slowing down our comprehension, blocking automatic reactions and raising questions even about obvious things. Unless there is an effort to turn oneself inside out, the Gospel is reduced to information and factual details. That's why things are said in parables—so that the person who thinks he understands won't understand at all. Rationalistic explanations, on the other hand, transform the message into slogans and render it inoffensive. The point is not to understand right away but to be understood, rid of all self-importance. The challenge that parables and paradoxes contain ought to be overcome—more precisely, accepted as an unmerited gift by a consciousness emptied of its own resources. The logic of the Gospel is aimed at small numbers. There is universal salvation, but it proceeds from one conscience to another. Every system of indoctrination or social pressure aimed at controlling people through their instinctive mass reactions contradicts the Gospel. We need to remember this. The Gospel of Mark leads to that of John— from first glance to internalization.

The paradox at the heart of the message is that the miracles are acts of power through which Jesus tries to reveal the humility and weakness of God. One can already foresee that the miracle of the Church—its power—will have meaning only when it is relinquished.

## The Vertical Instant

Passages, crossing frontiers—he doesn't have a home. Here you have no permanent dwelling. Time is short. On the move, always on the move—that's the way Mark sees him. From Galilee into Judea via Jericho, proceeding along the Jordan, coming and going. Mark isn't interested in history or geography but something else, which with the passage of time will be extracted from history like an invisible harvest. Jesus the nomad, on a level with desert wanderers. When he happens to go through his own country, his people don't recognize him. He said, "A prophet is not recognized in his own country, among his relatives, in his own home. . . . And if a place rejects you, shake its dust from your feet" (6:4–11). One must create large spaces within oneself, become a passer-by, a foreigner. He was unable to perform any miracles that day. Astonishing—his power was blocked.

One day they're on the road to Jerusalem, Jesus walking ahead by himself. The disciples are filled with awe; those following behind are afraid (10:32). Everything is summed up in that image of a man walking alone ahead of his disciples. Except for the women from Galilee who watch from afar, he'll be alone when they assassinate him. This constant tramping and crossing frontiers heralds other departures, other journeys, which will carry the Gospel beyond Palestine. It's always a matter of being uprooted. "Be not afraid." The whole thrust of the Bible has been in the same direction, ever since Abraham. *Exi*, set out. Every church will always be invited to give up its place. "If I don't go away, the Spirit will not come."

Quick snapshots: Never stopping on the road, not looking back. A few privileged moments forever inscribed in the flesh of memory— a heartbeat, the feeling of strangeness, a sudden breakdown, an uprooting, an awakening from which one must again awake. The narrator doesn't want to prove anything. He has no theories or fine rhetoric—perhaps that's why he touches me. His is a language both precise and breathless, his sequences more rhythmical than logical, and which disconcert us because they soar far beyond scholarship.

I, too, am weighed down with excess baggage, favorite quotations, a fear of being different, of being taken for an artist in an age of ideology. Nevertheless, miserable scribe that I am, there's an instinct in me stronger than my scruples as an ex-professor; there's a tone of voice I'd like to transmit, one my mother passed on to me without knowing it. It's in Mark's boldness, in the rhythm which sometimes, miraculously, comes through in certain translations, the sense of expectation, the violence of a joy that precedes thought.

The words of Jesus are those of a man on the go, filled with the color and odor of the fields, the wind in the trees, the gestures of ordinary people. Is it necessary to have been a peasant to understand, or to become natural again? His words invite us to become joyously present in the instant, like the brook constantly in search of the river, or the river en route to the sea. Look for the Father. Your neighbor is yourself, your unknown self. Non-duality is present everywhere. But Jesus' word remains unknown. We've scarcely begun to uncover its implications.

Perhaps now we can see better why, if his words had been written down or dictated without passing through the consciousness of different people who repeated them and edited them, we would have been enlightened but also coerced. Obedience would take the place of freedom and love. Certitude always runs the risk of hardening and finally destroying what can only ripen slowly in us, ripen and die in order to shoot up again. Words must emerge from the great anthropological roots we share in common, from each of us. So Jesus' word touches you like a hand on your shoulder, a threat as well as friendship, a fraternal and dangerous invitation that leads from the known world and the deciphered text and makes you cross over to a land that is both here and elsewhere, whose image you carry deep within you.

## The Necessary and the Impossible

No ideologist, eyes fixed on some restructuring of the world or the Omega point. When asked, "Who is my neighbor?" he responds (Lk 10:29–37) with the story of the good Samaritan. At the moment of truth each of us has to decide. Everything is at stake each time, a matter of life and death. Impossible to take shelter behind necessity. Stoicism becomes an empty facade.

A man went down from Jerusalem to Jericho . . . A man had two sons . . . We may let ourselves be lulled by the rhythm, but suddenly there's the punch line, something we never noticed before, and we no longer know what to think. The fatted calf is roasted for the disreputable son, the prostitute is you and me, caught up in society's universal prostitution. No neat chain of reasoning; a fundamental impulse sweeps away all objections. And it's not just a matter of parables. Jesus decides to feed the hungry crowd, moves to act on behalf of Naim's widow, weeps and opens Lazarus' tomb. To him, hands that reach out, eyes that weep, bodies that suffer, mean more than the ideas we use to get by, the neurosis of past and future. What matters is *here and now.*

It's impossible to wall up the word-parable without killing it. Of course, when it begins to grow in someone and becomes a central impulse, it can easily get mixed up with partisan prejudices. We should never surrender our critical sense. But the danger of simply being venerated, made a ritual to be observed, is worse—the same old refrain, offering comfort for smug consciences. But if the word is nourished and linked to the deepest needs of the individual, its energy is boundless.

What is upsetting about the story of the Samaritan who gets off his horse on the road from Jericho is that we might be led to think that it's enough to arrive after the battle, to nurse the sick and bury the dead. It's obvious that those who really work for justice in everyday situations and not just to create another form of oppression, struggling in the midst of ambiguity for a world with fewer dead and wounded, will not make as good an impression as the much-praised Samaritan. I know it's illusory to think that any society would ever be able to eliminate all forms of misery and horror; indeed, such a society would ultimately be inhuman. But how can we be on the side of the humiliated without taking action against the oppressors? Love cannot exist without anger. Don't we know that there is a type of love of the poor which is simply complicity with the structures of society that created poverty?

To love each other in God, in Christ, within the limits of a particular clan or class, while refusing to understand the influence of culture, money, and power—the consubstantial, almost invisible violence that is done to people every day—is relatively easy and can be done sincerely. All that's needed is to bow to the "evidence" offered by one's own prejudices or self-interest. Such love becomes harder when we take sides here and now, against what really prevents people from coming together—against the exploitation of work, the worldwide supermarket that dictates the law of the jungle. Because in that case a price must be paid.

To be blessed with faith can be simply the infantile happiness of someone who has placed limits on the Word and enclosed it in a cocoon. Someday it may crack. One truth stands out: Christian love is only a mockery if it doesn't strive in some way to make us *neighbors.*

To return to that withered and scandalous fig tree (Mt 21:19–21; Mk 11:13–20). Jesus and his disciples, who are hungry, pass by and approach the tree that isn't bearing any fruit. Jesus curses it, and in an instant it is shriveled to its roots. But Mark says it isn't the season for figs. This man, who constantly shifts from the intangible and the contingent to the absolute, doesn't seem to know what is reasonable and drags us toward the impossible.

And when he says, "What, you see the mote in your brother's eye; don't you notice the beam in your own?" (Mt 7:3–5; Lk 6:41–42), it's not just a matter of comparisons. That would simply mean accepting the mediocre wisdom of the world. It seems rather that at the very moment that I judge someone else, anyone at all, I become blind, whether or not I'm open to criticism by others. Those who judge others place themselves beyond communion.

It's in the same sense that we should understand Jesus' warning, "Whoever looks at a woman with lust has already committed adultery." Of course, he's referring to the Mosaic law regarding marriage, but the point of his teaching is directed elsewhere. After all, desire is part of human nature. Repression doesn't eliminate it but opens it to other more roundabout paths. Only boldness will change its character. Jesus doesn't see sin everywhere, even in our involuntary looks and thoughts. He means that one who has reached some degree of self-knowledge wouldn't know how to judge anyone, because the same impulses live in all of us. This is no encouragement for sin. The Gospel offers a broad vision because it is ontological, not legalistic, and presumes an openness to love beyond any calculation. In this sense morality doesn't exist for others, but only for oneself, a necessity because of a light that dwells within us. People are not lost or saved by either their goodness or their evil but because of the attitude they have to their goodness or evil. The just man proud of his virtue, of which he considers himself the proprietor, is as far away from the kingdom as someone who seeks pleasure outside its human context. Law is the substitute for goodness for anyone who doesn't spontaneously turn toward the good; in general such an approach merely conceals envy and an absence of love. So it is impossible to rely on appearances. "Judge not" has far-reaching implications. In the Gospel no one owns anyone or has rights over anyone. An ethics of rights can legitimately be based on necessity and social custom, but not on Jesus. As soon as we stop turning the Gospel into a pious book, insidiously reducing it to the level of our fears and dreams, the naked Word shatters the shell of formalism and the spirit of youth revives.

There is another example in the invitation to turn the other cheek (Mt 5:38; Lk 6:29), which has been the occasion for so many dense or ironical variations. It has generally been interpreted as a pardon imposed on the adversary as a final proof of superiority, but in the world inhabited by Jesus it is simply an appeal to the fraternity that exists in the universal foundation of things, far beyond categories of strength and weakness. According to Konrad Lorenz, even the wolf doesn't attack another wolf that bares its throat.

## A Coronary Won't Frighten Him

The lifestyle preferred by the Galilean is foreign to security as it is generally understood. People are obsessed with success and certainty. They thereby repress their deepest desire and their intimate truth, since sooner or later they have to submit to the pitiless examination which society insists upon before hiring them as extras in the theater of existence.

Whoever tries to break through the bars of his or her cage or even look through them is considered to be corrupting society, like Socrates.

If we pay attention to the New Testament, it's very hard to think that Jesus had definite opinions, that his ideas were organized according to a rigorous logic. His logic is interior. It is only commentators and exegetes who have transformed his sayings into a system that wouldn't overly upset existing mental categories.

Jesus was disconcerting, unclassifiable, hence an object of scandal. It was dangerous for him to disclose his identity, impossible, without risking death, to respond to the questionnaire that would give him a place in society: What is your country of origin? What degrees do you have? Are you Messiah or prophet? What is your income, your social security number?

He prays in the temple but announces its destruction. To say the things he says and not live as an anchorite but eat and drink with pleasure, to include women, publicans, and sinners in the company of his friends—what side is he on anyway? How could he avoid causing a disturbance?

What is he trying to achieve? No plan, although we now superimpose the word "strategy," wrongly and at cross-purposes. To destroy prejudices—that is, walls of self-satisfaction, to touch stony hearts, to make us turn toward the unknown Father. To awaken, to unveil, as if everything was already mysteriously present in us, as if it were simply a matter of opening our eyes and our hands, taking a step, and everything else would follow.

Jesus is driven neither by the ideologies nor by the hopes that arouse the masses, but he is with them on another level. Popes on horseback and diplomats who use their spiritual power to play politics are alien to him. So are Polish Catholics when on behalf of their religion they answer power with power. And yet he's on their side, and that of the communists as well, in the secret chamber of individual conscience.

He's for the disappearance of classes, not for class struggle. With the crowds, but against the mythologies that move them along like blind armies. Is he merely an individualist, then, totally disinterested in the fate of humanity? To change the hearts and minds of men and women one by one—that's what he seems, above all, to be looking for, but not by drawing on the collective myths of happiness, which arouse people for a little while only to leave them so completely to themselves that envy, war, and destitution always return.

Jesus is on the road with the prodigal son, and he's also with the father who waits on the hill for his son. Always on the side of the poor until they allow their greed to become a substitute for wealth, until they begin calling their taste for luxury and comfort justice. Never with the rich when they hold on to the money that gives them their dignity, the sharp sense of their legal morality, respect for the property of others, politeness, scrupulosity in small things, and almost all the virtues on the list, even charity. But with the rich when they are poor in spirit, when they consider their possessions nothing, when they have come to realize that their virtues are products and their law is merely the harnessing of desire.

Western civilization teaches us to grasp—to own/know/have power. Could it have survived otherwise? It all began with atrocities and wars. Only by an abuse of language can we speak of "Christian civilization." Christianity presupposes the violence of nature. Its truth implies a disruption of the mechanisms of instinct and predatory intelligence; it's a wounding of consciousness, the discovery of an inner space, another time. Jesus is teaching us to let go. Growth

49

doesn't interest him, nor the upward mobility of individuals, which always accompanies or follows money. His criterion for success is not the same as ours. He recommends descending the social ladder in order to find again the humility of the child (Mt 18:3). That's how the hierarchies of power and prestige are subverted.

Should this be understood as an action based on resentment? For a time I believed so. Nietzsche had entered my life and I interpreted certain texts in his terms. It's true, of course, that when, through lack of talent, aggressiveness, or courage, people are unable to acquire certain goods, they sometimes pretend to scorn them, deceiving both themselves and others. *Those grapes are too green.* They thus rediscover their inner equilibrium and reaffirm their self-esteem at little cost. Christians have not always escaped that trap. But Nietzsche deceives himself when he sees Jesus as driven by the resentment of the weak. His direct, naked glance cuts through appearances, sees poverty in wealth itself, and weakness in power.

Jesus is on the side of the marginalized, the immigrants, the victims of prejudice, no doubt about it. But his attitude is far from that of democratic good will; he's no bleeding heart. Can you see him, for example, like our shrewd modern bishops, trying to use democracy to impose Christian laws regarding divorce and abortion on non-Christians? As if Christian morality doesn't have to come to birth freely in each individual conscience!

The wealthy, whom he invites to give their goods away, are against him, but so are the unions, middle-class peasants and workers. In each case he only goes part of the way with them. But anyone whatever is welcome to receive his message, though he gives special attention to those whom history grinds into oblivion, the raw material with which nations fight their wars, their leaders constantly talking about the happiness of future generations while accepting the present sacrifices of the wretched of the earth.

For Jesus the worst folly would be passively fitting into a society presented as the only one that's possible and reasonable, but which insanely destroys, both psychologically and spiritually, both those who profit from it and those it eliminates.

What's the good of worrying about tomorrow? Tomorrow will take care of itself. From Jesus' point of view accumulation is crazy. There was once a rich man who had a fine harvest and thought to himself, "What am I to do? I have not enough room to store my crops." Then he said, "This is what I will do. I will pull down my barns, and build bigger ones, and I'll cram all my grain and my goods in them, and I will say to my soul: My soul, you have plenty of good things laid by for many years to come; take things easy, eat, drink, have a good time." But God said to him, "Fool! This very night you will be asked to surrender your soul" (Lk 12:16ff).

People have raved about some texts—when they weren't making fun of them. Consider the lilies of the field. Observe the birds of the air (Mt 6:26). What naive utopianism! How could anyone today give a moment's attention to stuff like that? The case is closed.

It's a question of foresight. Our relationship to God cuts across the computer, concrete planning, the monetary system, the class system. It's a question of the soul. Those involved in planning are summoned to interior detachment. It's a matter of spiritual freedom within farsightedness—the capacity to act with serenity while in the eye of the typhoon. How can we succeed in our warlike society, enter into the glory of this world, and call ourselves Christian, unless there is that secret inner zone that leaves us detached, although it can apparently compromise our immediate efficiency?

But why should it be easy to belong to both time and eternity? The world loves only what is its own (Jn 15:19).

Have you thought about it? He's just turned thirty. Neither cirrhosis of the liver nor arthritis nor hardening of the arteries is bothering him. Let not those who have been exhausted from infancy, the embittered, the resigned, and the skeptical invoke his name while remaining inert in their sublime or harsh purity, complaining how difficult it is to live.

An unhealthy mind never stops preaching about the vanity and alienation of all commitments. But haunted by the vanities it scorns, it is itself empty, adhering only to a dream. Such a mentality tries to extricate itself by means of symbolic words and actions that would dispense it from real experience. Placing its spiritual aspirations exclusively in the beyond, it unknowingly submits to worldly powers. That's how some people march ahead with one foot in each world and never stop cheating. Hoping to guarantee their relationship to God, they fail their neighbor.

Only one way to be a disciple—grow young again. That means learning how to die, to make oneself free, a traveler with almost no baggage. No acquired positions, no regrets, no decorations. Let the only dream of your life be—to wake up.

If he is condemned and executed, in the last analysis it is because he makes it clear that reforms and changes are not only to be made externally, but within ourselves. Such a message is unbearable.

Nevertheless, does the Gospel have something to say to the supermarket society that we have created? To find out, let's look at it with his eyes.

The West has lived and still lives on the myth of an inexhaustible nature and unlimited growth. The increase in the standard of living and happiness follows the rise of production; progress is automatic. Such is the dominant religion of these times of spiritual darkness.

Various unexpected developments—which we call crises to avoid recognizing that we've been living in permanent illusion—are beginning to reveal what traditional peoples were always aware of: the goods of this earth are limited. Let us not deceive ourselves: "Peace is another form of war." Various social groups, just like individuals, are struggling for the possession of these goods within our so-called advanced democracies, while half the third world suffers from hunger.

Societies, like individuals, live in a state of divorce from the earth, forgetting that its roots are also theirs. The pollution that is the result of this divorce is the symptom of spiritual asphyxia. Hold-ups, taking hostages, and all kinds of graft are only the most visible expression of an insatiable greed.

The need to exist qualitatively is not what moves most people but the desire to own and accumulate. There is a conspiracy to convince them that only quantity brings happiness. Television, advertising, and journalism aim above all at quantity; even books and ideas, like other products of our consumer society, have to submit to the prince of this world—money.

For a long time technology was only applied to our environment and to objects contributing to our material well-being. Now science and technology act together directly on our reflexes and thought-patterns, exploiting whatever is mechanical in our thinking, at the expense of our secret experience, the intelligence of the heart, and ultimately of liberty.

In the light of this fundamental discovery of the limits of the earth and its resources, it's extremely important to live and act with a different image of the world. Our rulers are only able to be referees, torn between the social groups that try, both within and beyond their boundaries, to grasp the largest share of profits. The process is endless. As in most revolutions, opposition groups generally aim only to redistribute wealth, without raising more basic questions about the relations between humanity and the earth.

In such a perspective, what political leader, even if a genius, regardless of party, would be able to propose and carry out a social reorganization that would genuinely respond to the common good? Unless he aims at his own downfall, his actions will inevitably be determined in the short run by divergent pressures and electoral demands. How could the power delegated to him bring about a new conception of the world when it can only be exercised in terms of immediate desires? He must rely on cleverness, a mixture of intelligence and a natural talent for deception.

We live in a state of darkness because contemporary societies understand salvation as simply the satisfaction of desires. If our lives have no spiritual foundation, why question this satisfaction? But the excess of desire, whether satisfied or frustrated, opens the way to sadness and inhumanity.

Everything is taking place as if the repression of eternity and hope was leading to a frenetic search for security in an effort to locate eternity in time.

It's hardly surprising that one of the most significant phenomena of our time is the denial of death. It's a menace that comes from elsewhere, a catastrophe that falls on us. Everything is done, to an absurd degree, to prolong life. We talk about respect for life while ignoring the fact that in many areas of the world the average life span is only thirty years.

The truth is that we no longer have the sense that the individual has a personal reality. You're mortal—so what? Production is immortal. Filed, spied on, manipulated, the individual is just raw material caught up in a program aimed at the future, based on polls and statistics. He is crammed with false hopes before being painlessly eliminated at dawn, unless he's prettied up in a funeral parlor, the better to deceive others.

Besides, people today are often dead before their time, as soon as they leave active life. Aid programs for the retired, the third world of the elderly—dramatize their abandonment by a society whose purpose is simply growth and pleasure. The unemployed, too, relegated to non-existence, have a foretaste of humiliation and death.

Societies organized in terms of scientific rationality are nothing but bookkeeping enterprises. That's why they fall under the law of the explainable, of platitudes and boredom.

Has the Gospel anything to say to this world of darkness?

To tell the truth, in the Gospel there is no darkness, or rather it is always dawn. Within our world given over to pseudo-scientific lunacy, numerous communities scattered over every continent are

53

even today creating a life of sharing and fraternity, a prophecy and a promise. They represent some of the most genuine expressions of the Gospel, revolutionary by virtue of renewing contact with ancient tradition.

Certainly, the Christian message in itself invites us to sobriety and reconciliation with the earth, but holds itself at a distance from economic and social realities. Don't decide too quickly that it's simply belief in the proximity of the parousia that explains this indifference. Salvation is not of this world, although it's an interior reality here and now. But it's not linked to progress, and is therefore not concerned with the transformation of the earth, and doesn't include, at least directly, any economic and social analysis.

Dare I say it? Yes: for someone who truly lives in terms of eternity, pain and death are only a brief passage. This is the kind of thing we generally don't want to hear anymore. Nevertheless, *only one thing is necessary*. There is a fantastic strength in faith, provided it doesn't remain a purely mental object, foreign to life.

For the servants of the Gospel cannot escape into idealistic refuges while leaving things as they are. Logically, they will seek to push back the powers of the inhuman, and will therefore commit themselves, each according to his or her charism, since the second commandment is like unto the first. Nevertheless, they are spared the frenzy both of immediate desires and their inhibitions. Their life is a life *with* death, the other name of God. This frees them because it relativizes things and leads to serenity in action.

Because the Gospel knows what human nature is like behind the veil of its pretenses, it can remind us that a system based on abundance and greed is radically deprived. As we come to recognize that the earth is finite, we discover an insatiable dissatisfaction in our hearts.

The liberation that the Gospel aims for is first of all interior, which is as true for the poor as the rich, and in the absence of that liberation all changes are only a matter of appearance.

This is neither conservative nor revolutionary. If, without illusions, the poor are preferred, it's because they are more apt, having nothing, to be open to hope. The Gospel doesn't know social justice as we know it; it deals with interior justice that can express itself only when we search for a social justice that doesn't confuse itself with economic expansion.

Turning excessive desires upside down on behalf of a salvation of another order, one that places us at the service of all that is humiliated—that is its path.

Those penetrated by its spirit will certainly not be able to dissociate themselves from political responsibilities and will be led to take collective national and international action. But they will not be content to be simply the arbiters of universal greed. They wish to offer another vision of the world, freed from the false rationality that is leading us to the absurd. Will they succeed? The world loves its desires and the catastrophes that follow them. And who has ever told the truth without encountering the cross?

## Father Unknown

After this brief digression into actuality, let's get back to Jesus.

The one who speaks to me through the copyists and editors of the Gospels can't be summed up by labels like sweet, humble, and wise, so useful in fitting him into the clerical vision of things, or by such terms as quick-tempered, imperious, or fickle.

Nevertheless, it is written, "I am sweet and humble of heart." It's true that beneath the anger we sense a zone of peace, as if even the violence was an effort to share, and had only one purpose—to lead us to the Father.

And when the peace and humility of the final week sets in, and, without people knowing why, Jesus, abandoning all prudence, goes up to Jerusalem, it's with a deliberate sweetness and humility that also seems like an attack. He decides to become a lamb.

His boldness is what is most striking. The force of the parables and paradoxes show it, the liveliness of his responses even more so, and the manner he has of dealing with questions indirectly and eliminating them. Where does he get his authority, this man who dares to overthrow the natural order of things? "You know that among the pagans their so-called rulers lord it over them, and their great men make their authority felt. This is not to happen among you. No; anyone who wants to become great among you must be your servant" (Mk 10:42–43). What audacity the man shows—if he's only a man—when he speaks to the Samaritan woman or invites himself to Zacchaeus' house. He is close to anger as he rebukes his disciples whose ability to connect ideas often seems deficient. When did they finally understand? What once happened constantly goes on happening. Human dullness will persist to the end. Shortly after the multiplication of the loaves, the apostles, who have forgotten to take provisions along, are worried. "Why are you talking about having no bread? Do you not yet understand? Are you unintelligent? Are your minds closed? Have you eyes that do not see, ears that do not hear?" (Mk 8:17–18).

Who is this man who asks us to have faith in him? "When the wind is from the south you say that it will be hot, and it is. Hypocrites! You know how to interpret the face of the earth and the sky. How is it you do not know how to interpret these times?" (Lk 12:55–56). He attacks head-on. What a claim he makes in his bluntness with Nathanael: "He who doesn't believe in me believes neither in this life nor in eternal life." Or when he says, "This world will pass away but my words will not pass away." This patient man becomes aroused as soon as it's a matter of idols and lies, not only when he drives money-changers out of the temple. To disciples overwhelmed by the splendor of the temple he says that there will not remain a stone upon a stone. His aggressiveness is complete: "Destroy this temple and in three days I will rebuild it. . . . And when you pray, do not pray like those pretenders who like to pray standing up in the synagogues or on street corners in order to be noticed by others. I tell you, they have already received their reward."

For years people have spoken of Jesus' attack on the scribes and Pharisees. In general we tend to denounce in others something that's also part of ourselves. It's a verbal game that's perfectly safe, allowing us to preserve self-esteem because we don't see ourselves accurately. In Jesus' case, however, it's obvious that we're dealing with something else. Matthew 22 has lost nothing of its power. Even after reading and rereading it, its violence remains amazing. This victim of assassination was also killed for his insolence, placing himself above the Torah, standing against the order of the most pious Jews, destroying their most sacred ties, saying to their face that they were cancelling God's word in the name of "tradition" (Mk 7:6–13).

The spirit of resolution and decision that men of action bring to business, Jesus applies to prejudice, closed minds, and customs, everything to which the powers-that-be are attached because they need sleep or the excitement of the crowd, depending on politics. "It is not peace I have come to bring but a sword" (Mt 10:34). "I have come to spread fire on earth. . . . He who lays his hand upon the plough and then looks back is not fit for the kingdom of God. . . . Leave the dead to bury the dead."

Making people laugh is dangerous. "Is it necessary to pay tribute to Caesar?" (Mk 12:14–15; Mt 12:15–22; Lk 20:20–26) It looks like our Lord is caught in a trap. If he says, "Pay," he's a collaborator and alienates the ordinary people; if he says "No," the Romans will react. Bring me a coin, Jesus says. Someone pulls one out of his pocket. "So you've got Roman money; you're making deals with Rome like everyone else." The crowd laughs; the situation is defused. This time humor pays off.

He speaks with such serenity of harmony and peace. But it's an armed peace that has been won after masks have been removed, wounds lanced, and conflicts overcome. It would be a sham to make use of his words to erect a purely mental, sentimental kingdom sheltered from harsh reality. The sword of his Word does not encourage escapism: "I have come to divide, to separate." He makes his attitude a model. "You will be dragged before governors and kings for my sake. . . . Do not be afraid of those who kill the body but cannot kill the soul" (Mt 10:17, 28). His words will be sealed with his blood. But it's hard to believe in the martyrdom of those who defend this or that worldly order just to protect the idealistic vision they've imposed on reality, or in the diplomatic virtue of those who use faith to avoid genuine challenges.

Jesus doesn't bother with such arrangements. For example, let the family defend its heritage, but keep Jesus out of the argument. Roman law is foreign to him. No one has a right over anyone, not even God who makes us his friends, as St. John tells us. Let the Establishment protect the family—that's their business, important, even crucial, a matter of flesh and blood. It's a way of domesticating people, encouraging the reproduction of their kind, limited to the conventional horizon of the tribe. But Jesus cares about fraternity and spirit. As Claudel says, "Spirit is not in the body; spirit contains the body and completely surrounds it." Jesus draws us beyond the universe of birth and death.

Who is this man who accepts us as we are, invites us to exist within chance and time, without hiding places or privileges, and yet beyond time?

Someone whose Father is unknown, beyond race and yet of one. Not the son of an ordinary household.

Our imagination and vanity make it impossible truly to encounter you. But it's easy when you tear us away from our worldly identity and heritage. You are the poor one, with no fixed address, constantly on the run, in agreement neither with those who want to create an order they claim is yours, nor with those filled with nostalgia about you. Constantly outside the circle that we draw, and yet with everyone in the midst of their errors and illusions, faithful and disturbing, like the cock's crow at dawn.

He is the one who awakens conscience, who pulls the world out of its rut at the end of a long march before it surrenders again to the weight of its load, whereas the political leader tries to keep things as they are, while announcing that they are changing.

Why doesn't he join up with the zealots? Why not call on the people to revolt? But Jesus is no agitator; something else is at stake. It's a matter of fertilizing consciences with inexhaustible words and acts so that over the centuries men and women will rise up fully awakened, tireless in building up the spiritual unity of the world by means of/in spite of all the imperialists, with/against all revolutions.

## Be Mother and Father as Briefly as Possible

Christmas is coming, and once again there is that sickening nostalgia. There are frosted fir trees, toy machine guns, parties that cost an immigrant's monthly wage, and all this under a flood of multi-colored lights, an insult to the world's poor. I know I'm being naive, but one doesn't choose one's anger.

I've got nothing against family feasts for the winter solstice. They are signs of health even if they build walls in order to keep everything more contained. Hope can grow there, too, and not just in that morning-after feeling.

But ultimately Christmas has nothing to do with these artificial and commercial delights. Sometimes we hear sermons that make the same point, but only a definite act would mean anything in this situation. Let churches be absent from these false joys; it would be a judgment, a streak of light.

I fear, however, that this is asking again for a miracle. Perhaps, after all, it's better to let the mystery survive in association with mockery. Jesus was lost and unknown twenty centuries ago, too, in the middle of worldly glories. It is up to "the poor" to choose him in the secret of their heart.

It hurts to leave the paradise of the womb, infancy, adolescence, a land. Put down roots, Athens says. Unplant yourself, Jerusalem says: let every land be a desert for you if you want to return.

Senile and imperialistic, such has been the family in history. Rarely present, turned to the future, devoted to entertainment, concerned to gather its members together, the family in itself opposes the free and joyous movement of life. How much time has been lost in struggles against the jealousy or ambition of fathers, or against maternal love!

58

What is born of the flesh is flesh, what is born of the Spirit is spirit (Jn 3:6). The family exists only in order to be transcended. Nature already brings us the talent and the wrench needed for our growth, for the harsh joy of here and now. The hour can come when we rejoice at the absence of what we love. If I don't go away, the Spirit will not come. Mary, it seems to me, becomes totally mother at the foot of the cross. Our loved ones inhabit us even more when they are dead.

Every child comes into existence with a unique style, inscribed in the very fibers of her body, a way of receiving the world through her eyes, ears, mouth and skin, of imitating it with her gestures and voice. Instinctively she rejects certain constraints, throws off diapers. People help free her so she can walk. Spiritual nature is more fragile. From the start the child has to defend herself against the reflexes, ideas, and dreams that people confer upon her, in which all the riches of experience are stored, of course, but also its fears. Later, if she has not been asphyxiated, she will be forced to break open the very vocabulary she has learned in order to rediscover innocence. It's a hard battle against convention, pre-judgment.

For people have presented a marvelous and terrifying gift to this child: spoken and written words, by which she enters the world of adults. A thick cloak of words encloses and represses the fleshly body to produce an adult who accepts elementary realism. Get established: if you want to exist, learn to dominate, possess. From the outset language invites the child to dissociate herself, making her live in opposition to her body and the world, not *with* it. In this way, whether we know it or not, we read death in everything and rush toward purposes which are not our own. An unhappy consciousness curls up in the hollow space between conventional phrases and the unique word that wants to cry out and cannot. Drugs, degraded forms of religion, nightmares, the obsession with success and fascination with pleasure—all try to fill up the distance and respond to the body's desire for epiphany.

The family seizes the individual and never leaves him alone, just like the society that overwhelms him. Its basic aim is to hem him in, enclose him in its ghetto, to integrate him. But if he is to give life to society and prevent it from petrifying, it is important that he become joyously himself.

Surely the sterility of most political commitment comes in part from the fact that it is a function of tribal men who act as functionaries, or even become insects unwilling to live today the free and happy existence they proclaim for tomorrow.

59

So what? Nothing is pre-established. Is this process inevitable? Each individual ought to tear himself away from the clan and the weight it has on him, and make his own truth conquer the inhuman. The Gospel is a plea for the essential solitude of a man or woman who genuinely wishes to meet others.

The family sometimes can become more than a hot-house of prejudices and slavery. Ties of spirit can become stronger than those of blood. That is its specifically Christian goal. In any case, the person who wakes up will sooner or later choose his own family, from which his relatives are not necessarily excluded.


Jesus has not blessed the family as such. His mission is to invite us to a rebirth in the spirit. It was the churches which, one fine day, placed themselves in the service of the species, increasing their power through the number of the baptized while simultaneously helping the authorities recruit soldiers, who were blessed along with their rifles, cannons, and bombs. In certain periods they undoubtedly helped preserve the family unit but the tension between the family and spiritual fraternity was not maintained. This was their failure, although some Christians always accepted this tension. The churches didn't hide the Gospel texts but a composite was produced. Faith became natural.

That the evangelists reported with such force and clarity words and acts which were not in agreement with their own thinking seems to me a powerful sign.

After choosing the apostles, Jesus lives a wandering life with them in fraternity. His family bustles about, gets upset, and tries to drag him away from such foolishness and hide him. Just read the text—it's quite obvious. *Who is my mother?* The exegetes, who for so long knew how to keep a close rein on what they were saying, give a fine account of themselves by exploiting Jesus' next words as a correction of his previous assertions: he who does the will of God, he is my brother, my sister, my mother. On that score the Virgin has nothing to worry about. But that doesn't change the fact that for the moment she is with his brothers and listens to the claims of blood relationship as if she still had to learn that the flesh doesn't count for anything (Jn 6:63). When Jesus declares, "Here are my brothers," Mark says that he looks around him; Mary isn't part of the group. How his family would like to shield him from death. They would never have let him climb Mount Calvary. His mother returns home that day alone, just as she will set out from the cross. Not that Jesus didn't love his mother. But what he wanted above all for us to know was that his mother was not loved because she is his mother but because she kept the Word.

Few of Jesus' words to his mother have been preserved; none is tender. The pattern was already established in the scene in the temple reported by Luke: "Why did you search for me? Did you not know . . . ?" And at Cana, when Mary says that they have no more wine, Jesus answers, "What is that to you and to me?" Of course, this Semitic phrase takes on meaning only through the tone with which it is said, which is perhaps simply that of easy friendship; after all, he gives in to her request. But he places himself at a distance. The words at Golgotha remain austere: "Woman, behold your son." The sentimental rhetoric that developed over the centuries has hardly any support in the Gospel.

That is Jesus' attitude to family bonds. Passing, provisional, they have to give way to others, which death itself cannot release. Like other founders of religion (with the exception of Mahomet), like Lao-Tse, Confucius, and Buddha, he's not very interested in blood relationships. Far from attacking marriage, he reminds us of the Mosaic law on the subject, but the center of his teaching is on something else. He risks his life by saying this in the very village where he had been brought up (Lk 4:16–30). If the cross that one sometimes still sees over the beds of married couples has a meaning, it's not the one people generally think of. Jesus thrusts the sword of his word at the exact point, between necessity and appeal. It is an appeal directed to all, in or out of families, expressing an attitude that challenges both natural habits and the law. If we have generally been confused, the Pharisees understood quickly: "We have a law, and according to this law he ought to die" (Jn 19:7). Don't assume too quickly that these were special circumstances; it is the spiritual order of things. Brother will betray brother (Mk 13:9ff). Blessed art thou when they shall insult you and persecute you (Mt 5:11). When tranquil Christian neighborhoods are held together by social pressures or political forces and you observe the prosperity of large tribes, it's not the Gospel that has been preached but prudence tinged with religion.


Blessings on happy childhood.

Nothing will ever replace for a child the experience of being completely loved by a father and mother. Let family life be intense but brief, aimed at healthy pain and new birth. For everything tends to substitute itself for the maternal womb in order to keep us in the cave of illusion: money, art, pleasure (when it leaves no place for joy), love (if it's only a remedy for boredom), religion (when it mollycoddles us), every memory, happy or unhappy, that walls us up within individuality. We are not yet born.

A divided family is hell. But there's something worse—a united family.

If you are a father or mother, be one as briefly as possible. Don't need your children too much in order to exist. They'll make you pay for it. Let the time come quickly when they choose you. Let your plans, worries, and good advice perish with you. Not all of you will see the year 2000, but your children will be in the best of health. To turn them into carbon copies of you is to assassinate them. That's why many of them fade away without saying a word, without even cursing. Nature arranges things properly so that sons often rise up against the wisdom of their fathers. There is too much docility and imitation: boredom will asphyxiate the world. Be secretly pleased, therefore, by your children's insolence, without pretending to be young yourself and without any favorable prejudice for that foolish stage of life.

A couple that experiences fidelity in the precariousness of the flesh, in both the absence and nearness of bodies, brings the only testimony of the absolute to our age of short-term markets. An enduring total love upsets the conventions, laughs at pretentiousness, and makes a couple both poor and all-powerful. But societies dedicated to unlimited growth, at least among certain groups, have made marriage a functional association to be exploited by advertisers for economic ends.

In this harsh world those who wish to experience a joyous love that would sustain existence must learn to become disinterested, place themselves at a distance, refuse false imperatives, and appear to be amateurs in the eyes of serious people because their real interest is in something else.

I'm speaking on your behalf.

Let those who are definitively in league with Mammon or the glory of this world continue to rush on into the torrent of illusion. But I'm speaking for those who haven't succeeded in strangling the dream of the absolute they had as eighteen year olds. Knock down the walls of the conjugal castle. Stop being bosses or servants of the international supermarket, perpetual worshipers or "ideal couples." Despite my own cowardice, I'm speaking, out of the childhood of the Gospel, a word that doesn't belong to me and that removes from love any notion of worldly hierarchy, domination, or possession. I know about the arguments which explain, justify, and weigh up the pros and cons; but they're just verbiage used to conceal the word.

I have never been able to believe that purity could be the product of some type of repression. The obsession with purity and sexual obsession express the same reality. Purity survives in the midst of and beyond the desire that is consummated.

Nevertheless, walking on 42nd Street in New York one day, past the porno film houses that project sequences outside in order to attract the crowd, past the peepshows and sex shops, I was surprised to find myself reciting the Hail Mary, flooded with joy at the thought of that woman conceived without sin.

Does it imply a disapproval of sex that Jesus escaped the everyday laws of reproduction and Joseph is on stage only as an extra holding a lily?

It seems rather that the meaning of sexuality does not easily emerge from the infra-human. According to Freud, the blind tendency of sex is to rediscover the world prior to sexual differentiation. Jesus invites his disciples to raise their eyes to the future and to desire, in the full light of knowledge, the same fulfillment.

In today's triumphantly pan-sexual world it suddenly seems splendid that human beings are able to reveal, despite risks and mockery, that love exists outside of sex.

*And at the hour of our death. Amen.* Death used to light up everything at the end of the Hail Mary. The humble prayer, which seemed only a refrain, was actually a challenge. Mary Immaculate invited us to live in the face of death, not to reject sex but its dictatorship. She stands for active expectation, the plan and the execution of a world of resurrection where it's not a question of dominating or devouring, and there are no longer either men or women, mothers or sons, in the womb of the universal body of love.


## A Veil Is Torn

Certainly, many of the moral intuitions of Jesus are already found in the Hebrew Bible, the Talmud, and the midrashic literature. Nevertheless, in addition to the unique, unsurpassable call to a love relationship transcending social conditioning, ignoring duties and merits and thereby shattering conformism, his language is new. Simple and calm, suddenly sharp, radical in the primary meaning of the term.

A veil is torn. You see beings and things in their nudity, which nobody previously knew how to speak of. Words become alive again; one would like to keep silent from now on, to remain pure in the sad, irrational flux of this world. There is a physics of the religious life,

63

with its own colors and movements, which is more important than meaning and syllables now that the absolute has been made flesh, living among people, absorbed by the elementary and deadening necessities of food, sleep, and reproduction.

Parables appear in quick, precise strokes. A parable is feeble; almost all the power is in the one who hears it. Fragile as a child who only has the strength of those who love her. Parables suggest a crisis, catch the moment when it's time to make a decision and act. The master returns from a voyage, the lost son is coming home, the feast is beginning. An invitation to a wedding. What's this kingdom they're talking about? No definition is given. Impossible and dangerous to objectify it. Let it remain in the dark since it has to grow in people's consciousness, be born of their love. Secret, a hidden treasure, it's unexpected, surprising. And we need to give up everything we have to gain it. A joyous discovery for some, catastrophe for others. Only one hope: to live in wakefulness.

Two moralities intersect. One seems to aim particularly at daily life, the kingdom of here and now. Here are found the poor, the abandoned, the suffering, the merciful, those who hunger for justice, the peacemakers, and the pure in heart. Neither the rich nor the powerful nor the pretentious know about it. But don't think it's a society of saints. Publicans are invited, the last are first, there's more joy over a repentant sinner than for the ninety-nine just. No room for observers of the law who forget what's essential to law, justice and mercy, who are the heirs of those who killed the prophets. The prostitutes will enter ahead of them. Nevertheless, any of them can suddenly topple into the kingdom.

The other morality looks ahead to the last day. Free yourself; the time is near. Useless to get married; blessed are those who make themselves eunuchs for the sake of the kingdom. Rid yourself of all goods, settle your lawsuits, for the day is arriving like a thief. But the end of the world is primarily interior, an ongoing process. Eschatological time doesn't take place on one date rather than another; it isn't held back by the barriers of centuries but breaks out every day. Jesus is returning this very instant.

The acceptance of evil, the absence of law courts, the renunciation of property, the overthrow of natural hierarchies—all this would mean chaos. That's why the evangelical counsels and certain precepts of Jesus became the preserve of monasteries. If realized politically, they would call into question the order of the world and certain ecclesiastical institutions which are its reflection. The Cathars, the

64

German peasants of the sixteenth century, and the Anabaptists were witnesses to a Gospel in such a state of freedom.

In itself religion is conservative; it emphasizes the fear of death, protection against evil, and a taste for the miraculous as an escape from reality. The Gospel, in contrast, implies constant revolution, rousing those who hear it from the sleep of fable and magic, as well as from any political absolute. It's impossible to choose; one must accept the tensions which are those of life.

## No Springtime in the Dry Wood

The parable of the wedding feast and the kingdom in Matthew 22 is shocking from beginning to end. It seems that when God issues an invitation we must respond. He sends his servants to call us to the wedding. He sends them out again. His insistence makes it impossible to live the happiness or unhappiness in which we thought ourselves sheltered. I come to the door and knock—an intrusive, intolerant king.

Since his messengers keep coming back to bother us, all we can do is get rid of them, along with his son. Verse 7 is too much; why this vengeance? Wouldn't it be enough to let the murderers finally discover their error? It's clear that Matthew wants us to connect Jesus' prediction of the coming destruction of Jerusalem with the refusal of the Jews, the first to be invited.

A third try. The call this time is without limits. Go out into the highways and bring back everyone you find. This time there's no summons at home; everyone is lined up, good or bad, without distinction. One might say that these new messengers are the apostles and their successors. There we are. All the techniques of collecting a crowd, for the glory of the king. And a fighting speech: you're free, but if you say no, you'll be cast into slavery and darkness. It's not surprising that someone is found—what's surprising is that it's only one—who isn't wearing the right clothes.

One feels sorry for the poor dope. How did you get in, friend, without coat-tail and tie? Let him be tied up like a bundle of sticks and cast into exterior darkness. The only justification I can find for such treatment is that he was already in darkness.

Jesus has just left the temple (Mt 24). As they walk along, the disciples ask themselves what he's thinking about. There is a connection between Jesus and the temple which only he recognizes. If the temple is that space reserved for a particular presence, where has God lived more than in the human space that is the body of Christ? The temple has served its time. Constantly destroyed and rebuilt, it was only a prophecy and should now surrender its place.

As Jesus turns his back on the temple, the disciples linger behind to contemplate it, fascinated by what has been superseded, like various versions of Christianity throughout history, like Lot's wife, who turned her face to look back on the fumes of Sodom and Gomorrah and was changed into stone. The loitering disciples, who have such a need of approval and acceptance, approach Jesus and invite him to turn back. His answer is incredible. . . . They would be better off contemplating the one who is walking with them, in whom all fullness resides. And is he not himself soon to be destroyed on behalf of another presence in the form of absence when, after time has been gathered in a flash, all novelty will only be mythology?

Arriving on the Mount of Olives, still upset by the predictions they have just heard, the disciples ask questions. When will all this take place? Jesus answers, but first describes, in the traditional style of such prophecies, all the calamities that are to come, harmonizing them with the fall of Jerusalem, which John (2:19) places in relationship to the passion. All the disasters of history, of the last days and of every day, orbit around that central disaster at the heart of history which gives them a sense of joy. You hear talk of wars and revolutions, epidemics, famines and earthquakes, but it's only the start of birth-pangs.

When is it going to happen? Simply asking that question is a worrisome sign. Look at the fig tree. Useless to watch the horizon or imagine the future. It happens when you're not thinking about it, when God appears, death's other name. Listen to the parable of the ten virgins, or the talents (Mt 25). To be expecting is not a matter of time but a disposition of the soul, a proof of love. Someone who doesn't give in to hope can never know the *unhoped for.* The man who loves no one expects nothing, is already dead. Let him be thrown into darkness; it's not a punishment, but the logic of life.


## *Hollow Out the Absolute*

One of the wisest men in history, the founder of Christianity—did he ever exist? This utopian who sees love as the ultimate goal, the redeemer who disdains pleasure, the socialist prophet who knew that the poor will possess the earth, the comforter of the weak and resentful? Who is this God whom the Church adores, using him to justify its attempt at domination, wielding secular power when circumstances allow, spiritual when it is no longer in control? Whoever he is, his seamless garment is still being torn apart.

It is good that he is not pointed out in dazzling clarity; in that way, his followers can choose him in their hearts. Maybe I'm talking this way only to console the child who believed so firmly in glory and to exalt the reality of a Jesus who is unknown and vilified. Nowadays I believe rather that a certain order of things emerges from every page of the Gospels.

I thought I might describe him in words; I even began to do so. Now I understand that it's impossible to separate him from the experience of his disciples. He breaks up the very language in which we try to enclose him.

Gentleness and violence, daring and humility. Peace-loving, except on Holy Thursday evening, when the apostles look for their swords, and he tells them two are enough. Maybe it's simply quiet humor, a disillusionment born of weariness. What's the point of explaining to them?

On one occasion he's bursting with activity and miracles seem to flow out of him; the next day he gets a poor reception and can't perform any. One day he announces the second coming; another time he knows neither the day nor the hour. He wants something now but the following day he doesn't want it anymore. He runs away from death, hides, goes toward it, accepts it; in St. John he pronounces heart-rending words of peace, and the next instant begins his agony. None of that upsets me anymore. The evangelists know as little about psychology as they do about history. Maybe we're just not told about the intermediary stages. Jesus does not understand notionally, or if he does it happens gradually, the way an artist is astonished or terrified by what happens in his work.

In actual fact there is no doctrine in the Gospels. There is an experience, a hesitant rhythm, which shows us a different God than the god of metaphysics, foreign to our mental logic, beyond the ways of power.

As a child I thought I understood that God was lowering himself. In brief, Jesus was pretending to act in a human way; he knew what he was doing, and was putting on a show for us. I saw no objection to all that since he was so powerful. At school one of my classmates, when he was asked what were Jesus' last words on the cross, replied: "I should worry, I should care; on the third day I'll rise again."

Is my present interpretation any better? Not if I hang on to it as a new form of knowledge. If he is that which is called God, he has no hidden motive and expresses himself in innocence. God cannot lie since he has no external appearance.

I am moving into a more secret zone. I'd like to stop playing superficial games, and enter into a second naiveté, even though I recognize the deceptions that this can involve. The character of Jesus, as it appears on the visible surface of the text, expresses the attitude and the ways of God. What used to surprise me, an irregular and uncertain style of thinking, is no longer an obstacle. I can see that it's not easy to communicate oneself in a contingent world, that Jesus does not quite know how to go about making men and women free, making them friends instead of followers. Which perhaps means that our tentative efforts, paradoxes and contradictions are also God's, translated into a body.

However, I'm not satisfied with that, as if I found it hard to admit that God could take the initiative out of the depths of his abundance. How are we supposed to understand that God is there to look after the human race? Moreover, how can anything exist outside of God if in some way God resembles our philosophical idea of him?

God is betrayed in reality, not in a scene from a play.

There is no need to know Jesus as an idea. Son of God—that means so many things in the Gospels and the history of religion. The disciples are astonished, stupefied by a man who is so out of the ordinary, a prophet in such a special relationship with One he calls Father—that's enough to begin with. They will know more about it only through the experience that will follow Easter.

Jesus' silence about his identity is also the Word of God. The tragedy is that many of today's self-confessed disciples, whose fervor is apparently more neurotic than mystical, should latch onto certain terms, whereas all through the Gospels Jesus turns all the reigning ideas about Messiah, Savior, and Son of God upside down. It is precisely through the deconstruction of prefabricated and idolatrous images, whose clarity is misleading, that the human characteristics of God are revealed.

Theology is to blame for having created a system that is sometimes narrowly legalistic, and sometimes as violent as a Western. One God has another God put to death in order to mollify his anger. Of course theology also tells us that he humbled himself, but despite all the nuances and distinctions, it's he who is pulling all the strings, presenting the rather strange image of a vindictive love and justice. Don't fool yourselves—a form of didactic theology still persists in people's minds. Read Diderot, for example, and you will see that he assimilated his pastor's sermons perfectly and drew his own conclusions. Contemporary unbelief still talks like him, which is far from unhealthy. As soon as we move away from the Gospel and spiritual experience, and follow either the old-fashioned or the new conceptual theology, we only drive attentive minds to indifference or denial.

The direct reading of the texts, even the form of the words used, can have meaning, inviting us to recognize that something is happening right now which also lasts forever. That through his temperament and in the events of his life and death Jesus gives expression to the *kenosis*—the unfathomable self-humiliation of God in himself, what Bulgakov calls "an eternal Golgotha." A wound bleeds at the heart of the absolute. No need to try to understand why God emerges. The theological idea of a plan which sees the human race simply as raw material no longer means anything to us. Incomprehensibly, God suffers at the same time as each human being who is the sign of pain and of joy. Jesus is what happens when God speaks freely in a man or woman.

## *Let the Word Penetrate Your Heart*

Let's stop for a minute on this sore point. I'm not concerned with small doctrinal distinctions but with ethics. Conventional theology is merely an outgrowth of the Gospel; when it tries to domesticate paradox, it only sinks into make-believe and idolatry. Breaking free from ideology, both before and during my rereading of the Gospels, is the story of my life.

The epiphany of the body, the incoercible desire for a perfect life, is inscribed in nature. The contempt and despair of a large part of contemporary thought is simply the passionate repression of that desire.

It's an impossible dream, since life endures only by virtue of the flow of creation, destruction, and re-creation. The Bible says that one must have confidence in the impossible. But desire has the power to arouse phantasms while creating parallel paths by which to escape the fear that is the other side of desire. Eternal life in the hereafter resolves the difficulty. But the Gospel doesn't invite us to that eternal life of nostalgia, in a white world of concepts. If eternity doesn't exist here, it has no reality at all there. Besides, all notions of space and time disappear. Saints, whether officially recognized or not, have not sought happiness merely in the hereafter, but in the kingdom here and now on behalf of concrete men and women who were their neighbors. They couldn't stand by, seeing evil and death reign, for they didn't know anything about the limits of the ego. If their language seems strange to us, it's because they don't share our idea of identity and because they express human unity in bodily rather than ideological terms. In the same way, artists, writers, and scholars worthy of the name don't sculpt, write, or carry on research in order to gain future glory but because of their need to create, to escape narrow limitations, to breathe deeply, and to express both their pain and a sense of abundance.

Above all, Jesus proclaims the transformation of mind and heart here and now.

Paul intensely felt the need to leave the shelter that submission to the law provided. He had come to realize that the law, although the expression of love, was also an obstacle. He has written some fiery pages about this. But our roots follow us, even when we are as passionately concerned with the interiorization of religion as Paul was. To some degree Paul's thought fell back into Mosaic archaisms, so that after rejecting Jewish law he replaced it with another law of the same type. Little by little, in the course of time, the accent will be placed on belief, ritual, law and miracle. Of course, the necessity of metanoia will not be forgotten. John's Gospel, which reacts against legalism and ritualism, will be proclaimed along with that of Paul. The mystical current will not die out but will be put to one side, a specialist approach suitable for monasteries, while faith will more and more become a system of salvation and an appeal to submission, especially after the Counter Reformation, when there was a hardening of formulas like *ex opere operato*.

In this way a split took place. Submission to law, even when interiorized by techniques of meditation and consciousness-raising (very much like behavioral conditioning), does not appease monsters; it only represses them. How can we remain true when, even if sincere, we think or act in terms of obligation—that is, what we feel we should think and do, not what we really are? That's how hypocrisy develops.

The illumination proposed by the Bible is directed above all at the conversion of one's mentality. It represents a liberation of the body and its reflexes. The word that enters through our ears descends into our heart before being expressed by our lips and our physical gestures. Such language is much like another, begun in Deuteronomy and finding its completion in the Gospel, and paradoxically in Saint Paul.

The God that we receive in childhood is never innocent. Moreover, neither is the refined God that we discover through experience and knowledge, if we don't detach ourselves from that knowledge.

In early childhood it was the miracle stories that fascinated me. I loved heroes who had special powers. The sick were cured, the dead came back to life, Roman soldiers were struck by lightning—Jesus was Superman. The enlarged catechism that my mother bought me so that I'd win a prize at my First Communion gave proofs for everything. But one day I stumbled on a question: Why didn't he cure everyone? What would have stopped him, since he was God? In the final analysis I was asking the same question as Hegel, whose ideas would later captivate me for a while.

According to Hegel, faith could only exist in universal terms. How could someone believe in the multiplication of loaves? Let him feed everyone or no one. It was absurd to bring one dead man back to life when everyone had to die! But we have to get beyond particular details if we are to understand Jesus' adventure. If he is born in a stable, it's because the Son of Man is first only a small, unintelligent animal. Little by little he becomes conscious of himself; he is presented to the doctors of the law who, after examining him, introduce him to the world of adults. One day he comes into conflict with society, which will destroy him because he refuses to submit to the requirements of civilization. Thus individual being, after passing through the perceptible world, is born to the spirit, the universal—*ecce homo.*

It's hardly surprising that so many eminent theologians became fascinated by Hegel, who was a great theological adventurer in the midst of a spiritual desert. In my case, a certain inaptitude for conceptual thinking detached me from him, even before I'd read Chestov. The Greeks, theology, and Hegel could never see that there is something more important than the Idea, or the immortality of the soul: the acts of a particular life, the concrete universal, the resurrection of the flesh.

And then I was struck by something else. The reality of evil is absurd only because we begin by imagining God in terms of human power. The accumulation of miracles on certain pages of the Gospel is misleading; in fact, they aren't very frequent. The Father communicates by abandon and silence, right up to Calvary itself. Although there are demonstrations of power, the whole Gospel is down-to-earth.

The miracles have nothing in common with the theater. As signs and anticipations of the time to come, that's already come, they can only be veiled and ambiguous. They occur when a certain tension of faith and love is produced in the hearts of men and women. A crack, a flash, breaks open the nothingness of appearances. It's like a guide at Vesuvius lighting a cigarette while all around gas and smoke are rising from the earth; he leans over and says, "Touch here, it's still warm." Miracles speak of the central fire. Glory exists within the bosom of annihilation, but is linked to it.

Golgotha cannot be separated from Tabor. Perhaps at the transfiguration Jesus wanted to comfort the disciples just before starting on the journey to Jerusalem. I believe that reality was revealed to them under two inseparable aspects, glory and weakness. One might say that majesty and lowliness are tearing at each other inside us and inside God.


## *I Go Away and I Am Coming*

It's difficult to speak of the passion—it's like making the person you're talking about remain silent.

How the West has reveled in the representation and contemplation of disaster. Painting, sculpture, the vast majority of monuments—except for those marked by oriental influences—as well as literature show an almost pathological fascination with the bloody battles waged for possession of the world, which prefigure the deportation camps, Hiroshima, and all the unfinished wars that we never tire of looking at and talking about.

I've never forgotten a conversation I had at the southern tip of India with a Hindu priest. In trying to characterize the West, he referred in the same sentence to Jesus Christ, Napoleon, Hitler, Truman, and Stalin. That was his perception of things; is ours less distorted?

The grandeur and terror of the passion gets most of our attention; the spectacular becomes more important than its interior meaning. It's hardly surprising that the TV news, which shows us other passions, mockeries and tortures in every part of the world, has turned Jesus' assassination into a legend, although for a Christian it is at the heart of human destiny and gives meaning to every agony.

Why did he decide to go to Jerusalem when he knew he was in extreme danger?

He is an adult whose fundamental intention, with all its demands, has remained intact since adolescence. As we see in the last chapters of John, he has reached his completion; from now on his physical presence would be only a screen or an obstacle to his work of bringing each of us back to our center.

His Word is directed at ordinary people and their desires. For a little while this accounts for his success. One person wants bread, a political solution, the restoration of Israel; another is looking for miracles or ecstasy, allowing herself to be carried along by the current. All hope their individual requests will be granted.

The hour comes when the word can no longer produce unanimity and it becomes necessary to face facts. He doesn't exactly want what we want, or at least he's hoping to achieve something else by means of it. Not political action directly but, above all, the transformation of minds and hearts; not miracles and ecstasy, but the faith and love that sometimes produces miracles. The conflict is obvious. Right from the start his word creates divisions, tearing individuals away from the crowd. It's not a matter of manipulation but of creating a new people that would make a choice against the physical law of numbers, against power. Hence it is a very small community that watches events from afar, condemned to not be heroic even if it wanted to.

If he had surrendered to the desire for immediate results—that is, if he had finally succumbed to the temptation in the desert—he would have become a political agitator, a military chief, and been eliminated by the Empire, like so many other anonymous rebels. Or if, against all probability, he had succeeded in mobilizing his hidden powers, the whole undertaking would have become absurd.

Judas betrays him out of disappointment, or does he secretly hope that the Galilean, once his back is to the wall, will show his power? Did he try to make a deal with the Sanhedrin and find himself overtaken by events? Was he himself betrayed by a Caiaphas irritated by the intransigence of a man he may have wanted to save? Judas no longer knows what he's doing. Hoping to help, he falls into the trap—which makes his suicide more understandable. Similarly, the words of friendship that Jesus addresses to him in two exchanges take on a more human meaning. They are addressed not to the obvious traitor but to the friend who is attempting the impossible.

But Peter too, in another sense, betrays him. As a realist, concerned with his salary and his glory, hoping to install his master on Mount Tabor surrounded by Elias and Moses, the kenosis has no attraction for him, unless there's no alternative. He has an innate sense of hierarchy and finds it hard to let Jesus wash his feet. But when Jesus tells him that he cannot otherwise have his place in the kingdom, he begs his master to also wash his head and his hands. At Caesarea, asked "Who do you say I am?" he has no hesitation. But as soon as everything is concentrated on the essential and Jesus says that he will have to suffer, be rejected, and killed, Peter says, "Fortunately, that won't happen to you." And Jesus responds: "Get thee behind me, Satan; your concern is for men, and not for God" (Mk 8; Mt 16).

Peter moves me. With his passionate love and his pathetic cleverness, he's always ready to fight, to compromise, or to pursue an ostrich-like policy because he is spontaneously drawn to glory and human success. The cock has often crowed. The Aramaic word *kephas*, Peter, has the same meaning as Caiaphas.

The history of twenty centuries is there in embryo. Peter and the Church with him—faithful, loving and betraying at the same time, unable to avoid betrayal because of their conception of things. What an incredible cavalcade of history, a marvelous, violent and scandalous epic, with Popes on horseback, the Crusades, love at the heart of a multitude, stronger than death, a time when entire peoples, in the midst of wars, plagues and famines, seem to experience with a kind of immanent knowledge a salvation that arouses the creative joy to which the first cathedrals bear witness! Then come increasing conceptualization and pretentiousness, the Inquisition, the emphasis on religion as spectacle, an enormous conditioning machine which tries to create Christian unity through external rather than internal means. Dostoevsky has sketched the image of the Grand Inquisitor for all time—it thunders with reality. But he does not see that deep down, both against and along with the imperial and doctrinal organization, carried along and nourished by it, humiliated love and holiness have always borne witness to the passion.

In one sense, as many have said, Peter, who was crucified with his head down, did everything upside down. But just as nothing could take place without Judas, it is necessary that Peter have his very human attitudes and that everything should take place in contradiction, seeing that this world endures.

Never have I realized so clearly that the passion is only a random news item. Jesus is the victim of hasty colonial justice, like so many men rounded up and eliminated before they knew what was happening to them.

A trial, like others. A small hearing. They talk about "the people" being present, but it was only a tiny fraction of the people, those who always attend this kind of show. The humility of the passion.

We think we know all the characters, but in the course of the adventure an unknown man appears on the road to Calvary, Simon of Cyrene, apparently a gardener.

And where does the resurrection start from? The tomb of an unknown man. Only Joseph of Arimathea has the courage to go and claim the body from Pilate.

Many are there who are not registered, are not present at formal meetings, but who come forward humbly and are thereby able to overhear the millennial word, or understand nothing and make gestures.

The fundamental reason why Jesus has to die makes the question of responsibility for his assassination pointless. Every society, Jewish or Gentile, that is founded on money, power, and law, condemns him. He puts people first, making economics and politics less important than men and women. In contrast, society, even when it says the opposite, deceiving others as well as itself, considers individuals simply as a means.

Simply to realize that the Word made flesh ends in the cry that every word repeats: *Eloi, Eloi, lama sabactani.*

The resurrection: properly speaking, neither a concept nor an historical event. To offer proofs is already a contradiction. Everything takes place as if he had to remove overly visible traces of the past in order to prevent us from turning back. But such a petrification has only partly been avoided.

Impossible presence. Presence involves the world, or the idols which are its projection, the frozen form of desire. Real presence. We should also speak of real absence. To find the word that would simultaneously communicate presence and absence, wounding with joy. If God were too easily present, how would we have managed to hold him back? Mystics know that God becomes presence in his absence.

The resurrection as knowledge, a fact to be believed, transforms faith into the categorical imperative. Jesus is only a miracle-man, and God is unavoidably something else.

To say that the resurrection was the *cause* of the disciples' faith is a partial betrayal. Paul speaks in that way, and through him the Greek way of thinking in mirror-images. It might be better to say that the resurrection is the expression of the disciples' faith. That which was external has become internal: love stronger than death.

To affirm a mental conviction is ambiguous, especially when it is passionate. Its connections and roots are too obvious. What is more important is the transformation of the way we look at things and our subsequent creative acts. The resurrection is a forward movement. Tomorrow at dawn Mary Magdalene is going to see him without immediately recognizing him. "Woman, whom are you looking for?" The disciples of Emmaus are setting out. People come together and remember him, not in order to return to a past that is over, but in order to live in the present, to create a new relationship in harmony with the word that leads them on a difficult path. What do we have to guide us? The sense of something missing, some uncertain yet sufficient clues that are a veiled proof for those who don't need proofs.


## Would You Like To Discard This World of Life and Death?

Before the feast of Passover Jesus, who had loved his friends, knowing that the hour had come to go to his Father, loved them until the end. . . . Let your hearts not be troubled . . . the world will no longer see me, but you will see that I live and you will live. . . . I do not call you servants but friends. . . . If you were of the world, the world would love what was its own. . . . You are sad but your heart will rejoice and no one will take away your joy. . . . Father, I do not pray you to take them out of the world but to keep them from harm. . . . I have given them the glory that you have given me in order that they may be one and that the world will know that you have sent me.

Read chapters 13 to 17 of John's Gospel, I beg you, and weep. Or rather, learn it by heart. To learn by heart is not what people think. It's an act of love born of intimate sharing which has a radiating effect on the rest of one's life, reuniting that which was scattered by the instability of things, gathering together the living and the dead.

John, who wanted to destroy the cities along the lakeside, the impetuous sinner who demanded the first places in heaven for himself and his brother, is alone now on an island but his heart is crowded; invaded by serenity, he lets his soul's blood run free. Faith is no longer black and white, a tension of the speculative mind. Light renders all things transparent. Which are Jesus' words, which are John's? What does it matter? Unity has been achieved. The style has become the rhythm of a living man who can express himself in Greek but who, in the semitic manner, first translates the movement of body and soul.

Here everything has become a repetition of an interior kingdom. Paul is preoccupied with propaganda and building up a large following. An astounding polemicist, he always returns to doctrine, treats the law like dirt while retrieving the situation for it. For John it's enough to live together and love; all explanations are pointless. One might say that for him doctrine and morality only exist in the consciences of men and women and in the experience of a new relationship.

There are some indications that John's Gospel is a reaction against the development of ritualism. Nevertheless, although he doesn't in-

76

clude an account of the Last Supper, the five chapters that include Jesus' last words would have no meaning without it.

One earth, a single body, of which we are members. We have no need of drugs to transcend the contingency of life; the bread and wine of our days are enough. Whoever you are, if you have faith and love, at that very instant you are what I am.

In the course of time the shared meal of comrades becomes ceremony and spectacle, a business. The Eucharist becomes another commodity on the market. The effect of spiritual gravitation is seen in the increasing concern for quality, leading to the development of behaviorist techniques, transforming what should be born of freedom and love into social obligation and categorical imperative. We begin to publish statistics and with complete seriousness pretend to calculate the level of individual faith. We announce that religion is declining in order to ignore the fact that what has disappeared is false pretenses. Passive obedience, once emphasized at the expense of responsibility, had for many years placed large numbers of people in a dishonest situation, and little by little they moved away. Some believed they had deserted the table of fellowship but often it was wounded love that separated them from a ritual which had become empty of meaning. Religious spokesmen talked about indifference at a time when many people believed they could find a more genuine fellowship elsewhere. What struggles some have to wage, what interior honesty they have to achieve, in order to adhere to the real (beyond everything that is called real), and what disappointments they have to undergo! But does it matter? For two thousand years the words have been pronounced over bread and wine, and in spite of formalism and hypocrisy, there have always been men and women who participated in his death and resurrection.

Claude Levi-Strauss, in his presentation of African and Amerindian myths, underlined the essential role of meals in human cultures. Communal sharing is also part of the primordial symbolism expressed in the Hebraic tradition.

Jesus brings about a change and enlargement of this tradition. By washing his disciples' feet he overturns natural hierarchies, cutting the history of the world in two. Part of every culture because of its tangible signs, the Eucharist proposes an unhoped-for response. Participation in the kenosis—the mystery of the annihilation of God in himself, in the Nothingness from which Glory emerges—anticipates the fraternal assembly of a future age, which has already begun in communion with the First-born from the dead.

"All of humanity since Adam," St. Augustine writes, "is the life of a single individual spread out in thousands of pieces over the earth." Hence there is neither male nor female, slave nor citizen, black nor white. . . . My kingdom is not of this world. My kingdom is not a spectacle; your roles are part of the script.

To overcome dualism and superficial realism, to wake up, to rise up from the dead, is to wipe out the barrier between sanity and madness and to leave behind the foolish distinction between the I and the non-I. Our natural perspectives are reversed: the eater is changed into what she eats, the student into what he learns. Beyond and through appearances, beyond the success and debris of capitalism, communism, and everything that conspires directly or indirectly to unity, the universal Body of love is being built up in secret. But history ignores the flesh and blood of Christ. The truth, Chestov reminds us, is what history doesn't notice.

Before acting politically, faith acts poetically. It creates a new way of seeing, it sings the Magnificat—that is, it overturns the powerful, lifts up the lowly, not because it needs to but out of a sudden realization. It sees strength in weakness, glory in the things that are ridiculed. The enormous absurdity of the cross shatters what the world calls reality. Truth is disarmed: it is a child in a manger, it arrives riding on a donkey, it hangs on a cross, returns from the night of death, and fades away after offering itself in the humility of bread and wine. This was the poem that was reality for the disciples, a mere fable for others. Who would not wish to take death upon herself, consume it, thereby existing in the joyous present, neither looking back nor ahead?

We are far removed from Western man, Roman to the marrow, with his juridical ideas of immortality. Posthumous existence in a legacy, a last will and testament to be opened only after my death, reincarnation in one's heir, in money set aside, hoarded, private property. This is my body, says Western man, contemplating his gold or what takes its place for him, his son, sometimes just before dying with the sacraments.

I don't know how it happens. No term seems right to me, neither transubstantiation nor transfinalization nor symbolism. Why should any one term satisfy us? There's no need to change the vocabulary. I adhere to the Word of mystery and poetry which carries out what it says.

Because meaning is not literal. One must have eyes to see, ears to hear. The paradox can't be intellectualized nor organized in the hope of domination. Concepts have nothing to add here; there is only the Word incarnate in an act. The absolute in bread, wine, the universal body. The dictatorship of reality is overthrown in favor of the secret and shocking truth. These lines on paper become a forest, this pebble on the grass is a star, this shell offers me the whole sea—metaphor, a touch of madness, a child's game. This is my body: the divine at play, the founding word of the incomprehensible play of infinite poverty. Why are you so solemn, fellow communicants? Why does the holy phantom so often replace the Holy Spirit?

The enlightened voices of our time cry out that there is no salvation, that there is only night under the empty splendor of stars, plus the absurd marvel of consciousness. They pretend to envy us, when they don't treat us as retarded. But their faith seems to make them more contented than ours. If they experience such despair in the form of stoicism, it's because they are still too drugged with hope.

All these passionate and sometimes bloody disputes that went on for centuries, about unleavened bread and bread with yeast, or communion under both species.

It's not bread and wine as such that are important but the basic food which sustains human life. It could just as well be rice or millet, corn, fermented honey, palm wine. It's through the nourishment of men and women that the universal body is created. The pulp of the invisible is in the tangible.

It's high time we finally begin to question ourselves regarding a dogmatic *a priori*. We have scarcely begun to realize that simply out of fidelity, in order to become what it is, the Eucharist should be expressed in visible signs that would speak authentically within African, Indian, and Asian cultures. This truth is repressed because it's painful to have to take a new look at the map of the world.

Why be surprised? Every language is old testament; the Spirit is buried under the letter. It's up to each generation to again give life to the metaphor.

And no illusions! Don't take me for a messenger, a crusader of the spiritual life. I pray, but my life lags behind, just like yours.

# IDEA

Up early day after day, I write this book because I can't do otherwise, without hoping to be understood, since ideology seems to have taken over. So often now Christians, both priests and lay people, publish position papers. Some, in a pathetic rejection of death, are turned to the past; identifying themselves with familiar truths and practices, they consider themselves "the faithful." Others make bold statements in a balanced, almost episcopal style; it's all a question of following the new wave and modernizing the doctrinal system. Still others station themselves at the frontiers, as pure as diamonds, bearing the image of a new community that would be totally committed to justice and would carry everything along by its own force. They don't always realize that they are the natural children of a Christianity of power.

All are obsessed with catching up with "the modern experience," as they say, or "contemporary man." In practice, they frequently go no further than the idea of an impressive organization that would automatically produce faith and love. Of course, they don't say that, they'd be horrified, but it's implied in their language. Between the illusion of the good old days and the illusion of progress and being up-to-date there is little difference. In order to live profoundly, in time outside of time, to be of every age, it would be necessary to leave so many things behind! All this makes for terrible bitterness between archconservatives and progressives, in a struggle that keeps their minds occupied and occasionally distracts the general public, while avoiding the real questions.

But here and there new communities emerge, small groups on the move, born out of a genuine experience, living out a vital new relationship. After a while myths are created, a certain ambiance. Then television is invited in, and people have the opportunity to uncover scandals among those who live openly in a world of spectators and hypocrites.

I write to keep up my courage and to respond to readers who've gotten in touch with me over the years because they thought they recognized a voice that also lived in them, and to others who have urged me to join the media circus and show where I stood in the "crisis." I want to repeat that there is no crisis. A few will be enlightened—those who already understand. Those for whom there is no distinction between faith and love, not only because they know that this distinction has no foundation in the New Testament but because they spontaneously consider the New Testament as a poem, a way of existing in the present. For whom faith is not a catalogue but the unseen sap that gives life to the tree. For whom the agony of the present situation is never anything but our fear of truth. Those who know that when God is confused with ideas he only represents nostalgia, and that we must cure ourselves of the desire of being everything and lording it over others. Some appease this desire with money, ambition, and vanity; others, sometimes simultaneously, with God and religion. This god has to be put to death, for the love of God. In creating men and women, God has consented to his own unending death in human consciousness. There's no end to death, from one person to the next, from one generation to the next. Humanity is like the animal that does not halt on the road to God. Death is the imagination of God, erasing only in order to recreate. In this way the quest for the infinite goes on forever.


Unknown companions for a few hours along the pathways of this book, I'd like to speak to you while the sea wind blows, bringing you back for an instant to that stranger who lives within you, and then *ciao*, have a good trip.

How can I speak of the heart of things? If I knew, there would no longer be anything to say. There is no heart. I will only say this: follow your deepest instinct. *Passion creates meaning*—on the condition that no calculations are introduced. . . . The authority of the word is absolute, but only in relation to a particular being. The fundamental error, the sin, is to make use of the absolute authority of the word without taking into consideration your concrete relationship to others. All reality is within you. Everything, good or bad, is for your spiritual creation as long as you don't remain outside of life, because outside of life there is nothing. If my wish has a meaning: may this book leave you broken and dispossessed, if you are not already, desperate for a joy you've never dreamed of.

Don't you feel awkward in your fancy words about eternity? You raise questions, you'd like someone to help you organize your ideas differently, you believe in answers. Well, go consult the specialists; they are masters in the art of embroidering lace on a void. Let's be serious: if you're lost in the labyrinth of conflicting truths, overwhelmed by the law, restrained by fear, stop this game, free yourself from faith itself. Live the joyous gift of today. Nothing is worse than boredom and sadness. Faith will not abandon you so easily; it's as persistent as crabgrass. During the era of Christendom it seemed useful to identify faith as a system of beliefs, but what was sociologically effective then is today a cause of failure. All it takes is for one thread to give way in the web of convictions. People don't really lose their faith, however; they merely recognize that it no longer possesses them.

It has too often been repeated that rejecting only one truth was enough to destroy faith. People who said it were convinced that belief happened in the head and not in the heart. But glances, everyday gestures, one's breath, a profound impulse—all these things express the truth of a person, with or without ideas. What keeps you alive?—that's the question. Keep yourself in a state of active anticipation.

I write every morning at daybreak. If language weren't so inadequate, I would have run out of things to say. But the Word never fails God, even though the very last words on the cross are words of abandonment.

How I'd like, for once, to make a book out of trees, water, roads, skyscrapers, crazy love, and poor people who march in the night, and let the Word speak for itself. The invisible in the visible, the absolute in the tangible, nothing else. Instead, it will seem that I'm trying to philosophize. If you only knew how little I cared about abstract syntheses and ideologies! But I promised to show you my way. It's one approach. *Andiamo.*

Every morning I write for you while the trucks roll into the city. If I wrote at noon or evening, moderation, that daughter of fatigue and fear, would guide my hand with a deadly sweetness. I have decided to place my confidence in the youth of morning. When we will no longer have anything but a small plot of earth to grow dandelions, there will still be mornings with their violent hopes. Everything is a beginning. I'm not trying very hard to pick up loose threads for fear that what I've already written should take over for me. Don't ask whether I'm repeating myself. I'm speaking about love. Don't look for order. Or look for order in yourself, in the heart of the source. But be suspicious of the order that passes directly into your head and to which you readily submit. Interior unity is infinitely stronger and more real than one born of logic and stylistic processes. Let the single dream of your life be to wake yourself up. Don't be stiff-necked, or I'll be forced to turn teacher and give you formulas.

## Prefer a Face

Many believers have read the declaration in Genesis that God made the world out of nothing, but they listened without hearing and are astonished that it could be something more than a metaphor. But every spiritual journey, although pursued on different paths, leads to

85

the discovery of the identity of the world and of appearances—that is, the recognition of the contingency and nothingness from which the visible emerges. Hence to lose oneself and to find oneself is the same operation. In ceasing to be a separate individual, you rediscover the dazzling wonderment of that which is in your own uniqueness. The real, or what people call real, floats over nothingness, but you gladly perceive its splendor and diversity, like a fireworks display that is constantly renewed, in the obscure awareness that the world is radiant only because it is both sign and promise.

> Daughters of Jerusalem, have you seen
> The one whom my heart loves? . . .
> Daughters of Jerusalem, I beseech you,
> If you find my beloved,
> That you inform him.
> For I am weak with love.

It is through the death lived in the instant that we can arrive at the invisible. The instant, the flash between two nights, before and after, the glow that life and death give off when they encounter, the constant dispossession. Without it we would be trapped by appearances. It is the radical insufficiency of words that makes them symbols.

Every genuine life passes through this second life, across joy and pain. What is this second life? The kingdom, *that* which makes life possible, joyous in every situation, beyond theism or atheism, something that cannot be justified, without why or how. If you haven't brushed against this experience, or don't have a sense that it is possible, you won't know what I'm talking about.

I'm letting you down. You were expecting something practical, ideas that you could rearrange as easily as railway cars, with the locomotive in front or in the rear, depending on circumstances. Instead I invite you to rediscover, beneath the cankered language of convention, your own breath. A single thought that arises spontaneously and plunges deeply enough into reality is enough to make us set out again in joy.

I invite you to stop hiding behind the abstract pyramids of ideas, or, when they collapse, to no longer wall yourself up in agony and bitterness. Hoping to embrace everything, everything escapes you; wanting to be everywhere, you are nowhere. Be suspicious of the absolute, the unsayable. Prefer a stone, a phrase, a face, which express the unsayable. When you hear someone speak of the beyond, tell him, "Only one life at a time!" When he speaks of the infinite, ask him how far he is willing to go to help people live or die.

86

Our griefs are doors, pathways for coming joys, on behalf of other sorrows, other joys. One sinks, the other gushes forth. Nothing is finished. Don't blame anyone—for example, someone who has hurt you badly. The function of morality is not to crush anyone; it exists only for itself. That there are laws and policemen is something quite different.

Stop looking for reasons, complaining that public morals are declining or that faith is dying. No, religion is doing very nicely; the archbishop is invited to dinner at the best homes. . . . When the sea seems to recede, it is breaking on other shores. Besides, the normal world is the pagan world of unbelief. Eroticism is natural; so is the love of money. Since evil is natural, let good grow within it and take its place. Complaining and protesting are only excuses for idle gossip.

I invite you, therefore, to maintain your distance. Preserve the unknown being that you are to yourself. Be wary of ideological structures which leave you empty at the very moment you imagine yourself fully involved. Ideas thrown out too quickly and accepted in the same spirit become insignificant. Better not to know exactly what you are giving or receiving. Expressing oneself doesn't mean wanting to communicate. Politicians communicate in order to pick up votes, businessmen in order to get orders. Avoid people who want to convince you of something. Not out of fear, but because of the noise.

There is an empty space to be passed through. The desert that you carry within you makes genuine encounter possible. What one person says exists only if it is recreated by another. Nothing is worse than overcharged enthusiasm, revelations, and spiritual gluttony. How can you meet in groups? They are necessary but it's advisable not to belong to them.

Let the wind blow freely among you, and keep your embraces brief. But each gesture, your very glance, should express your friendship, your taste for the real, and in the meantime your ardent patience.

## Faith Is Not Sectarian

Like everyone else, I want to have my say about "modern man." After all, I have dinner with him a couple of times a month. In an obscure way, we manage to fraternize. He has absolutely no interest in the idea of God and is more or less clear that it can only be the product of dishonesty. The world is composed of quantums of energy that have no special value or ultimate purpose. No one can ask anything of anyone. This modern man spontaneously rejects every support system, including the cult of pleasure and the joy that can come when pleasure is moderate. For him, every morality is the same since we all end up under four shovel-fuls of earth. No regrets or complaints. In the depth of his eyes I find a smile of recognition that removes pretension. One would sometimes be tempted to say that the benevolence, whether active or not, that believers find in thinking about God, he finds in the universality and proximity of death.

Nevertheless, for him the beliefs of Christians, which out of a need for security or a desire to defend a particular world view are associated with cultural representations of God or Jesus, provide a partial explanation for the disorder found in wealthy societies. To say that the only experience of God this man has is of his absence would be false. In any case, such a language would be meaningless for him. What fascinates me is that he seems cured of both ideology and guilt-feelings.

Certainly, Christians know that the Gospel makes demands on them, but only a small minority experience these demands from within. The others make an effort to be logical, while holding on to their aspirations or their scruples. What they adhere to, when they do, is only a system of thought that allows them to express their faith in a specific cultural context, and to harmonize it with the imperatives of economic growth, the sale of arms, repression, the race for success, escape into the future, worldly respectability, and a social morality identified with domestic justice, while notions of an after-life offer a vague background of dreams. Such a faith, pragmatically appropriate and never questioned, is both sincere and dishonest. Although it gives rise to arguments about "contemorary" problems, it is ultimately reassuring since it provokes no major conflicts with our consumer societies. This sort of Christianity, manipulated by today's audio-visual culture, seems the only kind that the "unbeliever" I've been describing is able to perceive. Needless to say, it presents him with no challenge.

We might well wonder whether this form of unbelief doesn't represent progress when compared to conventional faith, in the sense that it's more frank—an acceptance of the dark side of existence along with the taste for fellowship. We perhaps ought to prefer it to a faith that pretends to *obey* the Gospel when it surrenders to pressures and prejudices.

Only Christians who speak in a low voice or keep quiet can genuinely encounter these secular humanists for whom ideological faith, even when it's active and makes a lot of noise, is only a lazy cop-out. Such Christians no longer believe in the worldly importance of life, which is still tainted with religiosity, or in the values which give protection to the beasts of prey that manipulate our world, or in success and prestige. They'll never be honored by society.

It would be absurd to extol Jesus' mode of life, thought, and language for such people. There is an abyss between the Gospel, which has an affinity with the word spoken in the depths of everyone, whose basic ideas are interior freedom, universal sharing and communion, and the strange collection of bric-a-brac that weighs down the mentality of most believers. That odd assortment of ideas was passed on in random fashion by means of stereotyped and legalistic teaching. Creativity, when it emerged, was eliminated or brought into line.

All this was no conspiracy, just a powerful instinct to prevent spontaneity. A single model of thought and religious life was communicated to the rank and file by poor and humble men whose purpose was domination. The creation of parishes with the complicity of civil powers, the preaching of obligations under pain of sin and hell, with resulting guilt-feelings, gave these men a fantastic power. In a desire to eliminate superstition they cut religious life off from its roots in the soil; they gave in to impatience, ignoring Jesus' parable about the wheat and the cockle. They forgot that Jesus had de-sacralized religious observance for all time by showing that it is relative; out of a sincere love of the Gospel they tried to impose a totalitarian vision. By pushing rebels to the margins of society they prepared the way for secular thought to open up new perspectives on the human condition, thereby forcing faith to be seen in terms of its own definitions. The massive de-Christianization that followed was prepared by the process of Christianization itself.

Don't think I'm depressed. The purer a doctrine is, the more it creates its opposite. Everything—even love and holiness—takes place in contradiction and mockery. And don't assume that the process I referred to is over: de-Christianization is far from complete. In spite of the movement toward active tolerance, a logical consequence of faith that has not yet penetrated society in depth, if the institutional Church were to regain its members and its power, it would try to rule again, for the sake of humanity. The opening up in the Church has been less due to an interiorization of faith than a bitter capitulation; it stands ready to take over the reins again.

An abstract doctrine was taught along with a whole set of principles and obligations. This terrorist style of thinking, which fortunately was often mitigated by evangelical gentleness, addressed itself

89

to an unreal human being, theoretically determined by ideas, who was influenced more by fear than by love and was convinced that life's ultimate purpose could be reached only on a few highways that had been perfectly mapped out. No more footpaths, trails, short-cuts, in Galilee or anywhere else on the spiritual landscape, in the same way that mechanical progress destroys farmlands, trees, and roads in order to assure immediate profits. It was a period of theological slumber under the direction of professors, manipulators, and censors. The apostles slept, enclosed in their metaphysical shells, while the Son of Man suffered, a prisoner of the law.

That whole past—which is still present—can be found in religious manuals and literature, as well as painting, architecture, church statues, and sermons. Faith was expressed in terms of Western reason, an imperialistic procedure that divides everything up for utilitarian ends. Only saints and mystics were able to break through to a world of freedom and love. If it truly wants to be universal, Christianity has to become again what it really is.

Such was the naive discovery that got me started: it's not faith that is sectarian but the thought-structure in which it is expressed. To the degree that Palestinian and semitic symbolism has been crushed by Greek conceptualism and Roman legalism, Christianity is imperialistic, or in danger of again becoming so.

It was a matter of finding out if I was able to breathe easily again or to keep quiet while permanently exiling myself, whether within or outside the institution. I knew how to be silent. But I had stories to tell in a rhythm and a breathing which, I believe, communicated what was essential to anyone who knew how to read, who was more sensitive to the spoken text than to anecdotes. I would have preferred not to speak directly about faith or Christianity; it seems immodest. So for years I observed, sometimes with irritation, sometimes with amusement, the media presentation of "the spiritual crisis of our time." It's an illusion to think that, in the spiritual order, one has to enlighten the public, reveal its needs, and conceal scandal. What is needed is to create out of the depths of one's being, to give existence to one's faith. Nevertheless, a moment came when annoyance at appearing to dodge questions was stronger than the fear of becoming another voice in the concert of public opinion.

Why, although they pay reverence to the Word, do so many people seem to be ashamed of it? Hoping to make themselves understood in the worldly mode of communication, they research, analyze and criticize; they prepare the ground but they don't sow the grain of the word that emerges out of their own life. Perhaps they believe it's old-fashioned and couldn't take root in our sophisticated world. Nevertheless, the language of the Gospel, today as yesterday, doesn't refer only to its Aramaic cultural roots but to the universal, earthly origin of things—what Jousse called the primordial. Many regional entities today are trying to recover their roots, a healthy reaction against the false universalism of technology and ideology.

It's your way of speaking, something that's within you but doesn't issue only from you, since it exists beyond all the separate deposits of culture, and still remains to be rediscovered. It is poetry, a commitment, but not in the manner of media pronouncements. It neither explains nor demonstrates. It bears its proof within itself like the air that one breathes, like bread and wine, like a body close to yours, linked to the fundamental rhythms of breathing, of birth and death, arrival and departure.

So I'm obliged to say clearly how and why I abandoned a mode of thought which was familiar to me, as well as theology and philosophy. Not that I didn't enjoy meeting those two sisters; both gave me pleasure in my youth. I have no intention of attacking them. I'm telling the story of my life, that's all, a path taken among comrades.

## No System of Thought Is Respectable

After such an introduction my task may seem vain and pretentious. Pretentious because I dare to complain against a way of thinking that nourished me, although I never followed the path of scholarship. Vain because how can I express myself except by means of that very system? Don't complain too much if I still make use of the remains of dead ideas; during a monsoon the river carries along both rubbish and seeds.

I have to make you see that the Palestinian speech of the Gospel doesn't fit in with Greek conceptual thought. It's not a matter of rejecting one and endorsing the other, but of making you realize that the message of Jesus, when expressed in abstract doctrine, loses its substance.

Having reread the Gospel, I now want to consider its posterity. I don't expect there will be a great resemblance; what comes later is numerous and diverse. How could it be otherwise when Jesus withdraws and so many paths open up in later centuries.

The Gospels express the shock of an experience linked to gestures and the inflection of a voice, by people who didn't take notes or use a tape recorder. They present the same reality, the same word, unique and different, inexhaustible, nourished and recreated in the flesh of memory, spoken at random in particular circumstances by different individuals who, when they want to organize their anecdotes, fortunately have no intention of making every detail agree. They seem to foresee that the danger is not historical error, but facts that have congealed and become so removed from the warmth of life that all you can do is receive them in your head and repeat them while looking behind you, whereas what is important is to receive the Gospel with one's whole being, so that the Word will spring forth and gather together the body of God and the earth. The evangelists know that their guide is no longer within history and that the Spirit will suggest what is needed; they suspect that the commemoration and veneration of events could also be a betrayal. . . .

We should be especially aware that, despite the preparation for the Messiah so often mentioned—the anguish of a world that was breaking up, the expectation of salvation—the Gospel, in its first centuries of development, found itself at the heart of a totalitarian ideological empire to which it was radically foreign. For it is not by self-forgetfulness and love, especially the love of enemies, that one makes a mark in history. The revolution Jesus proposes is so utopian and crazy that you'd think its only hope is to slip into the imperial structures. Doubtless it survived thanks to its hierarchical reinforcement. At the same time, since it wanted to be universal, it tended to "objectify" the good news by recasting it in Greco-Roman language, emptying words of their original meaning at the risk of modifying the message through the pressure of vocabulary. How could such an intimate spiritual experience for a small group be expressed except in this language, unless it was content to remain the special privilege of a sect? How could the disciples of the early years of Christianity have offered a different image of universality?

Over the centuries the Christian community pursued a path of power. It resembled Peter, who had been similarly tempted from the beginning. It became thought of as more and more hazardous to let the Word make its own way within human consciousness. Thanks to heresies and councils, the message was saved from being absorbed into Gnosticism and was recentered at the heart of faith, but at the same time external unity was gradually substituted for interior unity. It tended to become a matter of will, obedience, and proclamation, transmitted like a cultural heritage. Faith became a thing in itself, a mental object. The day came when freedom of conscience, which had been insisted on during the time of persecution, was rejected in the name of faith, and the body of doctrine was definitively established.

So well established that there was nothing left to do but explain it, and impose what existed apart from the poem, apart from discovery—indeed, apart from intimate experience. The advantage was that Thomas Aquinas was not only a genius, but that he was dead. Hence we can simply write glosses on his text since he's already said everything. Even though he sometimes relied more on Aristotle than on Jesus, especially in regard to women, whom he considers hardly reasonable and to whom he assigns the purely technical role of reproduction. Of course, it's only one detail as against so many admirable metaphysical constructions. But suppose he had in fact said everything, since it's quite true that he understood a great deal? We need to remember Brice Parain's line, "that which has been said still remains to be said." When the Angelic Doctor declared that everything he had written was only straw, he was expressing his truth, the result of a mystical experience. But the authorities preferred to see this as a humble statement by a pious man and continued to make seminarians eat straw while claiming it was bread. Emptiness was avoided in the heaven of ideas by trying to keep the lid on that sparrow-hawk, the Holy Spirit. In this way a religious society was established that rejected pluralism and yielded to the temptation of an imperialistic unity.

To be fair, Peter (Kephas) never forgot one essential aspect of the message. During the Middle Ages the Church could have monopolized economic and military power for itself but didn't even consider it. Later we find the Church supreme in one place, with all powers at its disposal, and submissive and humiliated in another, but the demands of the Gospel are not concealed. Although interpreted in terms of established categories, its message remains intact, and is embraced totally by some mystics and theologians who accept the consequences. Tirelessly, the Church proclaims the very Word that places it under judgment. By spreading the message in doctrinal form over a wide area, by means of an overall system of techniques and pressures—through quantity to quality!—the institution offers both friends and enemies the means by which to compel it to respect the order of the Word.

It's not Thomism that annoys me but the way it was used, the way it's still used. In the hands of poets it reaches out beyond itself. Claudel's *The Satin Slipper* doesn't bother me any more than the mythology that lies behind the tragedies of Sophocles and Aeschylus. But no systematic thought should be given uncritical respect. The veneration people offer it estranges the presence it presumes. In the last analysis, it can only be suspected of concealing an absence. Only a constantly renewed creation can be a sign of life.

How difficult it is to analyze and criticize when one is dealing with such complex material that conveys both the best and the worst, with the worst sometimes giving rise to the best, and vice versa. Can you understand? Feel both anger and sadness and know that all is well. But that's no reason to be complacent. However pathetic our efforts, each of us must act as children of the kingdom.

## An Amazing Invention Against Death

If you are tempted to believe in God, beware of theologians and their conceptualizations. The best are the worst. But why are they called on to speak? Their roots are in an earlier age, while the Word arrives in its own time. Nevertheless, a few theologians emerge from the darkness, more poets and prophets than professionals, who bear within them the new image of a faith of "the poor."

Although perhaps useful and necessary, and a creator of history, conceptual theology is a great roadblock, constructed both with and against the Gospel and the Holy Spirit. It's not a work of impostors but of sincere disciples who have annexed God and Jesus and speak of transcendence while completely immersed in their own culture.

Art and culture have little in common. Culture is a compost pile, a humus that one looks after, smooths out, that one puts to use on a marked-out plot where everyone tramples on it. But art is only interested in itself. Solitary, it emerges from unexplored depths and lives on its own richness. It has no purpose except to harness its difference, which allows it to rejoin the universal. It has no answers. It exists in shadows. Don't ask it to improve anyone. It simply exists and invites us to exist.

In a similar way religious learning has little to do with faith. It puts ideas into some people's mental outlook and can produce automatic reflexes. It's especially useful when faith doesn't exist; it can take its place. In short, it reflects absence as much as presence. When faith emerges, religious culture becomes almost pointless, like the ground installations that make it possible to launch a rocket. Faith burns, creates the desert, and recreates everything in its own image.

I'm aware of the pleasure, like a cold burning sensation, of seeing ideas develop, of everything seeming to fit together. There is the

94

same shiver of excitement when an army passes by, an aesthetic intoxication achieved by the abstract absolute.

God venerated and dominated at the same time! As Spinoza writes, "Who can ever take away my ideas?" It's in that world of ideas that Fichte locates "the happy life." Until the day that the liberation offered by idealism is seen for what it is: a closed and sterile garden.

Do you know the story of the drunken man who crossed the Place de la Concorde at night? He knocked against the railing that surrounds the Obelisk and went round and round until morning; he thought he was locked in.

Except in the scientific and technical field, any constraint on thinking is already a deception. This is all the more true when it pretends to present God's message.


Conceptual thinking was an amazing development. Where would we be without it? We are indebted to it for science, bureaucratization, technology, modern comfort, and pollution. Countries that don't have those things aspire to them through a certain notion of happiness. In the world we have made, poetry has a hard time emerging. But we can still love our highways and airplanes, the cities that have been built against despair. On their walls, which temporarily cure our fears, doors and windows are painted that seem to open breaches in necessity.

But how can one deny that the concept allows us to analyze reality and act upon it? It has undoubtedly underlined certain potentialities of the Message, preventing it from being dissolved. Today, however, we are better able to appreciate its limits.

Every conceptual construction raised up against time tries to ignore the fragility of the body and the immediate instant. It keeps us from drifting by providing mental anchorage but doesn't touch us at that point where flesh and spirit are joined. "Thought is the daughter of fear," Chekhov says. That's why it goes so well with sadness. Instead of curing us of death through an interior experience, it represses it.

But if death is repressed, the resurrection becomes only an idea, a dream, or a wager that gives no life to existence. That's because in conceptualist thought the tangible and visible are only passing illusions. Even when it talks about faith and love it offers us only the eternity of abstraction.

The Greeks had a great longing for their native land. Ulysses embodies the odyssey of consciousness moving toward a place, a root-

95

edness, a temple, a vocabulary through which to look at the world, hiding its contingency.

The Palestinian story is marked by a fundamental uprooting: the exodus, the wandering of nomads. Time takes in its sails. You have no permanent dwelling-place.

Thought eliminates the body to reach the universal. The spoken or the written word penetrates to our anthropological foundations. One proceeds through the individual to the concrete universal, to the absolute in or through the tangible. The symbolic word begins by breaking open the conventional form of communication that only offers knowledge. To want to communicate is not to express oneself. Be willing to speak in the dark, perhaps to stammer. One takes what one can bear. He who has ears to hear. . . . Symbolic language laughs at preestablished meanings. It provokes a vibration, opens up a space. Both bold and humble, it doesn't pretend to wall in an inexpressible experience. A trace, a suggestion, it reveals and veils at the same time, makes us want to continue to search for its source. Instead of saying, "It's all in your head," from now on all you have to do is make an effort.

## Why Begin by Locking Yourself Up?

The concept is the perfect instrument for possessing the world, since it's an invitation to barricade oneself in the magic circle of representation, saying "Here is reality." In this way each individual is enclosed in his or her consciousness, even while talking about solidarity. Other individuals are only objects. The more we persist in making appeals for the poor, the aged, and the handicapped, the more they end up hopelessly enclosed in their solitude. God—the God of philosophers and scholars—is thereby placed at the service of man. Fitted into a technical mode of thinking, he is only a god-object, about whom people like to say he's long been dead.

Conceptual man is exiled from communion; death tears away from him the only thing that counts, possession. Exploit the earth for profit; invent machines to possess more. Cities are the fantastic creation of this desire to possess: constructed as a rejection of God, a substitute for paradise, they are nevertheless signs and promises. Those who manage to rule so well over the world—although it's always on the edge of chaos, straining toward indefinite progress, in flight toward the future—succeed only because they have repressed their interior life where the age-old voice still murmurs. The West with its mechanistic intelligence has thus become the third world of the spiritual life.

For a person with an interior life the idea of "progress" is just another ideology. Science, too, seems older. What endures is communion with the visible through the sacrament of the earth, an antidote to the poison of conceptualism; here there are no separate individuals. Life is a passage, exile and return, because of the alliance with "the God of Abraham, Isaac, and Jacob."

Why begin by splitting yourself up?

God, humanity, life—they aren't realities to be represented and interpreted. They are "in the beginning." We say "I believe in" but we're not "moved by." That's why joy rarely visits us, and when it comes we feel guilty.

But how can we find a way to live differently and get our bearings? We're anonymous and insignificant, isn't that it? We want a place, to be the owner, to have a name, to be someone's son or daughter, of a specific age, to have a job, an income, and a tombstone. Because eternal life doesn't run in your veins and you haven't learned to laugh, you have to feel important, like small gods. That's why, when you see everything returning to dust, you say life is absurd and abandon yourself to an adolescent revolt against death. Or you start taking drugs, of which the worst aren't those you think, but money and worldly success, which have much in common with a spiritual blindness that is masked by false virtues.

The despairing vision of the human condition proposed by some contemporary thinkers is the result of a childish disappointment with what was only a performance. Many people choose nothingness in much the same way that "believers" think they believe because they subscribe to certain doctrines. Let's have less pretense and accept the humility of the flesh through which our fragile hope is transmitted.

Concepts are an illusion, a palace of mirrors, a dream factory to compensate for the absence of deeds, an excuse for deserting the present.

Words can only suggest the physical earth, a bridge of vines over the abyss. Death, the other name of God; death, the great summer sun. The word "God," so impoverished and second-rate, as common as grass, bread or wine, has been congealed into an idea—the big boss, a slogan to put on bumper-stickers. What does it matter? God is the silence of every word. How can he avoid being absent? There is no other way of extending the limits of human ability. Imagine if God or Jesus could be said to be here or there, clearly pointed out. Everything would come to a stop. Without the great absence to be adored, life could never gush forth and burn itself out. Don't hide that absence with conceptual categories. God could just as easily be cruel as good, creator or destroyer, indifferent or infinitely attentive, joyous or a cripple. . . . Don't think I lack respect: I adore the divine weakness.

The God whose name cannot be pronounced, Y W H, exists when he is neither represented nor named. What is God? Ultimately, the question disappears. Silence is an answer when love in action shatters all speculation. For example the problem of evil is real only if you begin with the image of a God of love based on our human ideas of justice and love.

Nevertheless, let's not jump to conclusions. Those who have rejected God, we are told, experience the inhuman and fight against the impossible. I agree. But first let's have a little honesty. Is it so easy to forget about history and some of the effects of belief?

The truth is that when God is affirmed and adored, men and women can be enslaved. The proof of this is seen when our thoughts and actions become an official performance.

The same conceptual image that people shape for themselves makes some believers, others unbelievers. But in its highest realm Christianity stands above the opposition between being and non-being, which express two different aspects of the reverse side of God.

Thinking has wavered between these two poles: God as Creator of man; man, creator and destroyer of God.

Bultmann writes that God means "the disavowal of the human enterprise, doubt, and judgment; for Gogarten God is "the absolute crisis of humanity."

A change is taking place. "Human freedom" is no longer debated but left to silence and experience. The question has been eliminated, and God is considered irrelevant. It's hardly surprising that some Christians seem to be deserters, like those priests who aren't really priests, those apostles who aren't apostles, those believers who don't look like believers, who silently bring a response to life that is neither "moral" nor "religious" nor ideological. If you remove your blinkers, you will see the unpronounceable name blazing in their eyes. No, it's not blazing; it's a tender hidden gleam.

God manifests himself where he is not in fact named, without any precise reference-point or assurance, in a creative impulse, in new relationships. At least such a reading of experience is possible. Silence about God shows our disillusionment with language. It may also involve cowardice and laziness. Nevertheless, it's finally a question of language in the sense that destroying words is a way to purify the way we see and to unfetter the way we feel.

## Jesus Was Silent

A brief encounter with Edwige. A student of Arabic, she has changed her name to Hadewijch. She's an intellectual, trained in philosophy and theology. For years she's been on the verge of suicide. She's a tangle of questions and contradictions, but for the past year she's been at peace, in harmony with the Bible and the Koran.

This is the kind of thing one finds in the "Spiritual Letters" of Hadewijch of Anvers:

> Don't neglect any work
> and don't do anything special
>
> Be kind and compassionate in every calamity
> and don't take care of anyone
>
> May God bring you to understand what I mean
> in the one and simple essence of love

"Love is all," she writes. "Neither my heart nor soul nor senses are at rest, not even for one hour; its flame never stops burning in the marrow of my being."

I've always had two kinds of readers. Some are primarily concerned with subject matter and are astonished or scandalized by the somber stories that my books seem to present in colloquial, irreverent language. They are often the same people who were impressed by my first books, which were more nostalgic. And there are others, who read me with their lips, who breathe in unison with me, and tell me that I help them survive.

In my desire to be brief I haven't told the whole truth about how I got into literature. Because of the admiration I had for the writers for *Nouvelle Revue Française* in its great days, I took up writing with the intention of composing beautifully polished novels or essays, of creating complex, lively cultural objects for contemplation, in which the writer pretends to be absent. Mirrors. An elegant and lofty aestheticism—something that could be read with one's eyes, composed for the pleasure of a detached intelligence. And in the background as

99

motivation, the stupid idea of glory and posterity that school and TV puts in the hearts of French boys and girls. To speak, some day, from that pedestal.

With so many images and ideas in my skull I apply myself to be like the great writers I admired. I have a little success, begin to get recognition, even win a few prizes. I keep going. The polished objects crack, my fine passages get all mixed up, living faces begin to obsess me, and a word emerges that breaks the harmony. Imagination seemed like child's play, a pathetic entertainment for fashionable women. My vanity survived but my hope of glory was destroyed. The concern for posterity is a false lure, a terrible absence. It's here, now, that glory exists, in this tiny fragment, each instant of life, death, and resurrection. Where does the word come from? That's not my problem: I trust it. That's what I've tried to say.

From the start I feel close to all those whom society has marginalized—tramps, addicts, freaks, even "establishment" types, empty of spiritual substance and beginning to realize it. They live in the midst of steel, glass high-rises, highways that have become cemeteries, sex shops, and the rubble of human failure. But at the same time I notice with amazement that a song of freedom flows through everything, a paradoxical joy more powerful than my pain and mediocrity, the hope which those who bear it within them say they recognize.

What is surprising is that when I first began to write, skeptical and anxious to imitate others, believers in general applauded me. Now that hope plays her music in me, carelessly mingling with an existence that is simultaneously horrifying and wonderful, some believers just switch off.

Precisely because the word is immemorial and timeless, it can only be expressed in the instant. To remain in a dream of the past or the realm of ideas is to compromise with death. Since the absolute has become incarnate, how can one not be present at each moment of time, with its particular style, in the uncertain, irrational and painful flux of life, as well as in the bright lights of cities and in every human creation, in order to reveal that perhaps there are cells of purity even in the midst of Vanity Fair and that all things conspire toward unity and joy? Not to be contemporary leads inevitably to betrayal.

Sunday at five, at Notre Dame for an organ recital by Cochereau. The organ stopped suddenly and I didn't recognize Cochereau's touch. A priest wearing an alb seemed overwhelmed behind the pulpit. He began to speak, tourists walked in and out, and I was seized by the pity of it all. The priest raised his voice—I heard him refer to social conflicts, the religious crisis, the oil shortage. This holy man was using elegant rhetoric to preach to sad old people and a few holy Joes. When will the clergy realize that they're not being asked for their ideas about society or the current crisis or the future of Catholic Action, but for a word from him who rose from the dead?

Easter, with a mixture of snow and rain. The South Vietnamese are retreating; we see clusters of people clinging to boats and planes, trails of corpses along the highways. At noon the Pope speaks, blesses the crowd in color, *urbi et orbi,* and people applaud in St. Peter's Square. Oh God!

In the evening there is a debate about Jesus with representative personalities from Judaism, Protestantism, Marxism, and Catholicism. One speaker says he never existed; another, that it's not absolutely certain but myth, too, represents reality. Another begins by raising questions about language. The debate takes place in a church. The whole thing is a mistake. We see in the background faces of ordinary people, confused or saddened. Among the debaters there is one serene face, a person who remains silent. His eyes speak. *Jesus also remained silent.* The official spokesman of the dominant religion, his presence gave a kind of absolution to the masquerade.

The next morning I obtained his phone number. He seemed pleased and sheepish, having just been given a dressing-down by some big shot for not speaking up at the debate. He asked me if I would tell the big shot what I thought. He must be joking.

## Sing a New Song

The message of the Gospel can come alive only in a mind that is timeless and therefore contemporary. Today it grows weak from using a fabricated and authoritarian language. The Word of faith is confused with analyses and commentaries.

Because it was born in an Aramaic and semitic culture, where language is concrete and the tone of voice is primary, some feared that the Gospel was linked to a particular locality and that only the triumphalist thought of Greece and the West would allow it to become universal. But this tradition has produced very diverse fruits. It has expressed the universal in terms of science and technology, and in ideologies which poorly camouflage the appetite and will for power. In reality, Christianity, once it becomes linked to abstract thought, merely skims over the surface; genuine universalism is concrete and has to have roots. On key matters Aramaic culture is much like Celtic and African culture, as in and all those areas where there is a common anthropological base of instincts, gestures and language in which the spiritual life is linked to the senses through birth, bread, wine, and death.

There's a long road ahead for those who try to follow the Gospel. It calls for demanding discipline, along with the renunciation of artificial universalism and false cultural wealth in order to rediscover the humble language of the poor. It's an invitation to be reinserted not simply in one's native soil but also in the soil of cities where people have their roots, however slender, and where the millennial word is proclaimed above the din of the media. Once again Christianity is invited to turn things upside down by rejecting the loud voice of imperialism.

To hold two positions at once. To battle for language, since this is to battle for the spiritual life. At the same time, not to uproot anyone's vocabulary. The important thing is not to stop en route; as Malebranche says, "to have enough movement within oneself to go still further." To be intransigent, and yet to recognize that the humblest old lady who knows her catechism by heart can have a conversation with angels.


It may be that without firm structures or the ability to cross the frontiers of the empire without a passport, the Christian community would have remained a sect, and that without a solidly constructed body of thought the Gospel would have crumbled. But the means has become the obstacle. The map of the world is no longer the same. We know more about the meaning of language, which in its diversity expresses the body of the earth. The historical process of organizing thoughts in order to communicate them from the outside, like a garment of words hung over different cultures, is like the individual attitude of someone who hangs onto dead ideas with an infantilism that has nothing to do with the spirit of childhood.

Like many people today, I followed an arid road. One day I recognized that I didn't know what I was saying when I spoke, sometimes with authority, sometimes with passionate conviction. It seems to me that obscurity and loss of status have given me back my freedom and a new faith at the same time, even though I well understand that it's constantly necessary to struggle against one's own ideas. Because it's impossible to stop without cheating. It's fatigue that makes us put definitive words on what we were looking for and say "I've got it."

Imagine believing that what comes first are the ideas and appearances which impregnate the mind, and that one only catches up with the "real" afterward. "A movement," Engels writes, "begins in an idea." That's certainly true in politics, and we see very well where ideas in that realm often lead, what slavery they produce, and not only in the People's Democracies. But it's not the human or spiritual approach. We will never catch up with real people unless we start with the body of the earth, which is also our body.

Nevertheless, it's certainly necessary to leave our birthplace and the garment of language that covers and oppresses us. To understand the theater where we play our parts and use a borrowed language— what else can we do? But realize that it is theater. And even if we continue to perform, realize that there are other theaters, as well as a world where one no longer has to play a role, where one is fully alive.

There is a time for a borrowed, tranquil vision, for everyone and no one, for knowledge, confinement in an invisible shell, with joy painted on our faces—sincerely painted because we believe we are in top form. And another time to be wounded, to laugh at having believed we had encountered God, to blush at having said it, to enter a kind of nakedness in discovering the artificiality of ideas that we had imagined were part of us. And in this way to begin to exist in a more relaxed style, more available to the first comer. You can be like someone who all his life shouted out his faith, which he believed was his own, and suddenly, perhaps at death's door, realizes that he is surrounded by darkness and asks himself, "Have I been lying?" Better to wake up before you're laid out for burial. Someone who believed he was in the desert, discovering new lands, asks himself if he hasn't simply followed his natural instinct for comfort. . . . There is no spiritual life which does not encounter deception and disillusionment, suffering and confusion.

So it must be repeated, the memory of Jesus can be merely a glance behind, sincere veneration of a past that we see ourselves reintroducing into a life sprinkled with pious thoughts and symbolic acts. But we will always have to go through the disappointment and disillusionment of Golgotha and the ascension. To remember is to experience him as alive here and now in the unknown and to laugh at learned theories about the empty tomb, the appearances, and all that archaeological material with which people distract themselves; it means coming out in the open and creating a new relationship. Because as soon as that happens, it relativizes all the ideas, old and new, that we have or thought we had.

## Don't Be Fooled by Appearances

But let's not go running off into fideism and begin having visions. Faith isn't delirium. If believers who escape into metaphysical speculation make me think of sexologists who have never experienced joy and take pleasure in imagining pleasure, those who fly off into lyricism about the love of Jesus, despite all the sympathy I have for them, tend to confirm the skeptic who lives within me.

I don't believe in dogmas; I adhere to that which underlies dogmas and is their source. I mean that I don't consider the formulation of dogmas as an absolute; they became more of an obstacle than a means a long time ago. Who would want to drink at a dried-up spring? In the spiritual order everything is spontaneity and beginning. Whenever doctrine becomes solidified—whatever the need for some kind of formulation—it transforms weak people into slaves, the strong into revolutionaries, and leaves the others indifferent. Faith is not communicated by means of doctrine only, but in spite of and apart from it, to everyone who believes that something opens up beyond human experience.

Don't think I'm scornful of rules and rituals—they're necessary even for games. Otherwise we'd adopt other rituals and even more pitiless laws. But in the last analysis neither laws nor rituals create love; they imply it. The death of Jesus radically challenges for all times those social mechanisms that substitute culpability or repression for love. "All men naturally hate each other," Pascal says. "People have used desire to serve the common good, but it's just a pretense, a false image of charity; ultimately, it is only hatred." One has to want to be a dupe to believe that love can be harmonized with worldly prudence and good will, with the "virtues" that help arrange our comfort or a "justice" that is nothing but the organization of universal greed.

Reverse Dostoevsky's formula: "If God exists, am I still in control?" You're certainly the boss if God doesn't exist. Worldly hierarchies, social morality, and the police take God's place, and are especially implacable in countries where he is radically denied. Whereas if God exists you're no longer in charge.

To return to the essential. All *knowledge* creates distance. Language is the impossible and necessary attempt to repair the fracture, a bridge thrown up between the representation the subject gives of itself and the object itself.

Traditional theology has certainly not gone as far as Hegel in his attempt to remove scandal from the experience of Jesus but, though centered on grace and freedom, because of its origin in Greek thought it was determined to reduce the event, particular, unclassifiable and unexpected, to the large generalization. The result was that God, submitted to reason and logic, possessed every quality except life, and Law and Order could rule again. In this way faith became quasi-*natural*. That which has been could not avoid existing again, with the result that consciences one hoped to liberate were imprisoned in still another necessity. And so countless believers of good will strolled about in their closed heavenly garden saying, "Come join us, brothers; we are living the true life, the only happiness." If they had only looked around a little, or could have listened to themselves!


In contrast to faith as knowledge, faith that is experience and word immediately gives us the reality that it aims at, the way a poem does. What is separated in reflection is not necessarily separate in reality, though knowledge always tends to dry up living forces.

Reason can lead someone in good mental health to the edge of the irrational, come to a decision about the unknown, efface itself, and yield to faith. At that point there's an end to speculation within faith itself, since such discourse is a defense against self-effacement—that is, against death.

Get rid of the idea that secularism has prevented the Gospel from getting through to people. It's the rationalism that was introduced into the message, making it an abstract, imperialistic ideology, that undermined it. Nevertheless, reason retains a key role, not to speculate on the unknown and "transcendental" object with the hidden intention of dominating, but because of its critical function. For we must also get rid of the idea that reason is anaesthetized by faith. A faith which produces fear or sleep is a false faith.

From the start reason fulfills its function by not surrendering too quickly to the irrational out of impatience or fatigue; in other words, by agreeing not to use God to remedy the weaknesses of reality. Jacob's wrestling with the angel ends only at dawn. In addition, reason recognizes that no choice is made once and for all. The person who has awakened is still sleepy. That is why reason remains on guard to detect imperceptible slips. It is concerned to control the reality of commitment, but not by the coherence of thought or the fervor of sentiment. Because to sing the Credo is not necessarily to live the faith. The naiveté of faith can be as crafty as speculative faith.

We must abandon the scientistic idea of objective fact. For example, what is the resurrection for the disciple? There is an empty tomb and some stories about apparitions. There is no decisive fact. This fragility is linked to the central mystery of Jesus. We're invited to search more deeply. "Have you seen the one whom my heart loves?" The element of the unknown in the resurrection is like an aspiring emptiness. Everything is involved in it—the Holy Spirit, the Church—from different civilizations, expressing the same inexhaustible faith. The very vulnerability of its proofs gives faith its essential character, which is to be incapable of being possessed. There resides the paradox of divine poverty that withdraws in order to let in history, liberty, and love.

It's not faith that keeps insisting on irrefutable proofs, but a denatured kind of faith that can be passed on by propaganda.

The accusation of subjectivism has often been used to justify intellectual imperialism while simultaneously concealing spiritual emptiness. The *object* of faith is not a means of knowing, any more than the mystery of Christ is an object of historical knowledge. We can't reach it across twenty centuries of history, but faith instantaneously makes it contemporary. Hence it represents neither *object* nor an effort to understand but the transformation of the subject. Of course, it remains a human act; the movement that leads to adoration is intelligible. Nevertheless, all dialectic fades away. Thoughts by themselves have never produced a single act of love. They proceed or accompany such acts but do not create them. What reason discovers at the frontier of the absolute is precisely that the absolute is not an object of knowledge.

Becoming a Christian, therefore, is not the act of super-reason giving its full attention to a transcendental super-object. Otherwise, how would it ever free us from duality and introduce us to joyous communion? So much energy has been wasted by specialists studying the religious object. They might better have dedicated themselves to the analysis of human reality and to uncovering illusions; perhaps the world would then be a little less inhuman. When I hear them sometimes, always with sad faces, still leading discussion back to the object (or the content) of faith as if they'd captured it and put it in a box, they make me think of shopkeepers on the brink of bankruptcy. I'm reminded of a page of Péguy: "I'm not asking you what

106

you say; I'm asking you how you say it. . . . It's the tone, the style, the resonance of what you say—that's what I'm looking for."

## *"Let Thoughts Share in the Freedom of God's Children"*

So much that we call understanding can develop into make-believe. Even in the order of human knowledge, to understand is often simply a matter of putting a new word among words that are already known. To take an example from a field in which I'm no specialist, if someone speaks of tachyon and explains that it's an element whose speed exceeds that of light, I tell him that I understand. Or if I hear "persec" and I'm informed that it's a unit of distance among astronomers equal to 3.26 light years, again I understand—or imagine that I do—because I think I know about light. I have no desire or ability to investigate further; I have neither the time nor the inclination.

It's the same, even more so, when it comes to eternal things. The natural tendency is to come to a stop at signs, with a pretense at understanding that shows laziness and pretension. For example, the concept of a personal God in itself, apart from a spiritual experience, is only a projection into metaphysical space of someone who has a high opinion of himself and passionately desires to be immortal. Everything gets organized on that basis. If God exists, he is all-powerful, all-good, etc. Hence, if there is disorder, man is guilty. Such a God must reward and punish. This is the kind of irrefutable logic that forms the foundation of many religious consciences. Religious knowledge is often only a shriveled chain of reasoning that starts with an idea that can't be questioned, the recognition of the need for a solid foundation.

To understand? It's not so much a question of understanding as of being projected beyond oneself. Otherwise, how could that wider love break forth, giving us such joy when we discover that we are *understood?* Language cannot be distinct from the person speaking; one might even say that language creates the speaker. It's not primarily discourse about something but action that's needed. I surrender myself to it and I either receive or am restrained; it's a constant struggle. Among many of the living dead language continues to function by itself.

The Christian world has often attacked scientism but there is also a Christian scientism. It extracts information about God, man, and the world and builds up a body of knowledge which is all the more powerful because it's considered the Word of God. A class of specialists organizes this material while popularizers make it widely available. This knowledge then becomes the property of a class that holds the keys to it. How would such a process fail to create a world of followers and imitators whenever it's not completely rejected as a foreign body? In this way religious thought is always in the past, archaeological even when it's modern—a funeral pyramid, as Hegel said.

I have nothing against knowledge and its order when it doesn't kill all creativity. If I challenge knowledge, it's because I hardly have any. But if I were rich and had an enormous reserve in my barns, how could I resist believing in it? What would remain of me if I were stripped of it?

One can be impressed by the marvels of contemporary science and technology, take pride in our common humanity, and yet realize that the exploration of the planets is only a spectacular entertainment, and prefer the Book of Job and some pages of Dostoevsky, which represent a far more significant exploration.

There exists a primordial faith, the direct perception of limits and nothingness, which is an opening to the absolute and the impossible. When this perception doesn't exist, Christian faith has something artificial and foreign about it. And it doesn't always exist among specialists. Christian thinking of this kind aims at communion but begins by separating. It cites poets but is not poetic; it comments on but fails to give us the Word in a tangible body of language. Although it speaks of becoming rooted, it is not rooted in the flesh. "Let your thoughts," Goethe writes, "run towards us like God's free children, crying 'Here we are.' " How far we are from that grace! Teilhard appears as an erratic prodigy in the desert of Christian expression because he is, above all, a poet. It's not, however, the poet or the man of meditation, whose letters raise questions about his own theories, that we listen to, but the ideologue, because he offers a total explanation tinged with science. Christian intellectuals say to themselves, "How wonderful! One can be a believer and still be intelligent."

This is what's tragic. Some become thoughtful and say to themselves, "What do ordinary people need? What should we say to the men and women of our time?" But they have to experience the need themselves; they have to suffer, find their own approach, their own word. All religious discourse is empty if it does not present its proof in a breathing body. Unless you're convinced that faith is only an assent to propositions and not an existential experience in which the message is grasped with your bare hands. And that the community of proclamation and explanation has been definitively substituted for the living and confessing community. And that the interior kingdom promised by the Gospel is only a lure, and that it's enough to obey, watch, and wait.

It's significant that at a time when apophatism has all but deserted the Christian world, it finds asylum among writers like Rilke, Blake, and Holderlin, or that it forces its way into the heart of an anti-Christian philosophy like that of Nietzsche, just as it exists today in scattered form among those who write in despair and mockery. Those who live on the boundaries between blasphemy and adoration are sometimes more stimulating than the machines that produce religious propaganda for today's fashions.

Every militant faith expressed in the language of official demonstration and "conviction" only produces an atheism to combat it. In fact, such atheism hopes to occupy the same place that "faith" holds. But as we have seen, there is also another atheism which refuses the label, its eyes open on nothingness, and which creates a new manner of being in the world. To this atheism must come the response of adult faith, a reflection directly linked to the interior Word and the Gospel, in discreet communion, a naked thought, outside truth, in quest of God beyond God. It's hardly surprising that people sometimes accuse the most searching figures of our day of compromising with unbelief. Beyond the declared community, they are in search of a more profound and universal community. They shatter the circle of security in order to rediscover the living source that can break the ice of the long winter.

## Watch Your Language

Words travel a long way, perhaps because they aren't, of themselves, bearers of reality. They contain the truth like a jewel-case holds a diamond. "God," "faith," and "love" contain as little truth as other words. Both means and obstacles, words lie as much as they tell the truth. They have only the strength of our feelings and the warmth of our comradeship.

To let ourselves be convinced that there are truths "beyond" us and pretend to venerate them—that's how to evade reality. We live in a time when everything is devoured by information, the acquisition of superficial knowledge at the expense of creative interiority. Words are utilized, whether sincerely or not, in order to escape the demands they imply. But many people never ask themselves these questions and are content. They jump to defend their false security by speaking against modernism or new fads. They want to believe—

and have others believe—that faith itself is attacked if someone questions the authenticity of their faith. But truth and love can only be gained at the expense of illusions. It is said, "You will have to answer for every idle word that you pronounce." Must we keep quiet in order to lie less? But everything can become a deception. Even the purity of silence.

Every word implies a choice, a point of view, a judgment, and describes a reality that's part of another order. The question is: How can we prevent words from completely replacing what they signify?

Many people, whether knowingly or not, have spent their lives thinking it was enough to adjust words, to use memory and intelligence so that words would end up growing in individual consciousness. That's not true, not in the spiritual order. Someone who merely transcribes and transmits, repeating words and ideas without rewarming them in the heat of individual consciousness, without a process of re-creation, is only the mouthpiece of the dead. Someone who merely writes glosses or manipulates commonplaces may proclaim the incarnation and the resurrection—but he denies them at the same time.

Maybe it's inevitable and even necessary for human intelligence to detach itself and organize the metaphysical substructure of the Holy Spirit. To believe that it's enough for the specialist to discover a rich vein, and all that's left to be done is to coin it in the practical language of social communication—that's the academic approach to the transmission of a message. The only word that's delivered in that manner is a dead word.

Dead truth is worse than error; at least you can react against error.

The word of Scripture or the word of someone who proclaims the Gospel anew, the same yet different, reaches us with body and soul intact. There is the shock of a superabundant life with its burden of enigma and its secret, which draws us toward the risk of adventure.

A spiritual message passes from one consciousness to another through the vibration of an existence, in a single gesture, a single word. As soon as ideas are extracted from it and formulated in theses, they put us to sleep and produce rejection.

It's impossible to cheat reality. Reality will always take its revenge. The abandonment of the Church, indifference, the much-publicized religious crisis, are undoubtedly related to the new structures of society which no longer have credibility. It's not that there is less faith but that sociological conditions are changing. That's true, but to an incalculable degree those structures are also the crystalization of our illusions and lies.

To become aware of the abyss that separates words and reality, to live with that pain, is to pray and thereby reduce the split, regardless of the poverty of words.

Ultimately, words need to be fulfilled. For it's not verbalization that best brings people together, but something more obscure and vital, a breath, an aspiration, a movement, gestures, that make people who have different opinions recognize each other. Even among those who use the same vocabulary and the same ideas, if that quality doesn't exist, a declaration of community is only a veil of illusion.

Nothing is worse than confusing the absolute with a verbal statement, which is only a stuffed absolute, a mirror-play of the mind. When we think we rule over the absolute we only evoke a ghost. Fortunately, this finally becomes evident.

If doctrine has attracted so many commentators and coaches, the whole parasitic race that substitutes itself for creators and prophets, it's because they wanted to build the tower of Babel with words and ideas. As far as individuals are concerned, it was also due to nostalgia for the past, the result of fear and hatred of life. Since people are not always inhabited by the superabundant life of faith and the joy that goes with it, they surrender all the more quickly to the urge to convince others. At the same time, however, although they employ the traditional phraseology of proselytism, some are able to communicate a genuine presence. But of itself all religious discourse, because it's overly concerned to lock everything up, dispenses us from paying attention to it. It provides the cure along with the pain. Its function is to soothe, even when it condemns and denounces.

The thrust of the Word can only be borne in the hollow of consciousness, without any detour. Loves offers no explanations or proofs. It takes you by surprise, disorganizing before recreating; it invents its own path, the path of communion.

## From the Tangible to the Immaterial

Do you understand?

You only have the right to speak about the grain of truth that grows within you. You can't talk about faith as if it's something outside of you, a kind of spiritual satellite that turns around in the heaven of ideas. The gift of tongues takes place only in the depths of a living experience. It's the authorities—though they're no longer the *authors* of anything—who make us believe that abstract thought exists. This allows them to treat us like posts or girders in a prefabricated structure. It's not the living who imagine that faith is disappearing and morality is crumbling, but the dead. Whether they realize it or not, such people consider morality and faith as a product, and men and women simply as supports for a human construction.

It's silly to believe that what is needed are elaborate explanations, that the problem is to clarify what is obscure. There's no *ex opere operato* in language. Don't confuse the liturgical text and the word, which is *ex opere operantis*. If a person wants to be something more than the mouthpiece of the dead, she must let the Word percolate within her until it emerges, the same and different.

Stop locking yourself in your skin like an animal in a cage. The word-poem doesn't get just into one's head but stirs body-consciousness into movement, like a roar of laughter. To be so-and-so, with such-and-such a character, so many years old, with this particular job—all that is meaningless except for Social Security and the tax collector. To get out of oneself, to rediscover oneself, is the same thing—it's connecting up with the universal. Absolute and silent within us, the word splits open the world of contradictory desires, tries to break past the barriers of egoism, expresses itself in bursts of anger and joy, revolt and prayer, and acts out a dance. It's like the preverbal stage of childhood when you found it hard to distinguish your body from the body of life, when you didn't exist as a separate individual.

To create literature is to give life. Not just the appearance of life, the immediacy of experience, or the imitation of life as a distraction. But that element in life that is carried along and nourished by it, consumed in the fire of consciousness, consubstantial to the soul, transformed into words of resurrection.

When Rimbaud writes

O seasons, O castles
What soul is without fault!

he is juxtaposing two disconnected verses. Nevertheless, he really is dealing with the division of the year, springtimes, summers, perhaps a particular summer, a particular winter, all winters, all summers. And the castles stand for all castles—strong castles, sand castles, the castles of the Loire, castles of cards, castles in Spain; seasons and castles become images stripped of their materiality, capable of penetrating the heart of consciousness, with their burden of nostalgia for changing seasons and the perfection of castles. And here you are with your inadequacy, your fragility, delivered over to time and death. The presence of a kingdom emerges between the lines.

Just as in art and literature, the real, or what we call real, is grasped by those who give such unique expression to it that each authentic creator can be immediately recognized in a page, a single phrase, one canvas. Just as a child recasts the world in his or her uniqueness before being harnessed for useful purposes, each Christian "author" only knows how to speak in his or her own voice.

I realize that there is something scandalous in this for those contemporaries for whom everything is just a combination of fashionable ideas and packaging. And I also realize that the implication is that genuine apostles have hardly ever spoken out. Nevertheless, this is the direction in which we must proceed. In societies where people exist only in terms of their profitability, the vocation of Christianity is to remind them, against all evidence, of their royalty.

I'm looking for an individual, theologian, exegete, if possible a complete scholar. Someone like that Buddhist monk who said, "If I happened to meet God and he told me, 'I'm perfect and all-powerful,' I'd hit him over the head with a stick and throw the corpse to the dogs." Humor should be part of Christian language. Along with freedom of thought, irony, a laughter that would slowly break things up, adoration that would come as a great blast of wind, a language that would reduce the separation between knowledge and esthetics, between faith and human acts, that would open up to the beyond. There is a future for such a theology; may its time come soon.

Truths for our feet
Truths that can dance.

## Are You Humble?

I have to give a lecture at Saint-Louis-des-Françis. The man from what used to be called the Holy Office is in the first row—an attentive, rather friendly face. He gives the appearance of being amused: go on talking, my good man.

Every time I have occasion to speak in public about a religious, literary or philosophical subject, when it's in a didactic style for a large audience, everything goes well. Ideas fit together like the pieces of a jigsaw puzzle. I listen to myself speaking: delicate lies, maneuvers to forestall objections, bold phrases that are retracted in the next sentence. It feels like prostitution. Words present themselves as if on parade, just those that are appropriate—unless one has been so imprudent as to drink too much wine at dinner before the affair. There's almost total approval of what I say; people like objectivity. Except for the handful of my readers who wait for me as I'm leaving to ask, "What got into you?"

When, confident that the audience has already been won over, I act without strings and unburden myself of my convictions, hesitations and doubts, refusing to manipulate ideas and remaining as close as possible to my experience, I generally sense disapproval. "What a confused and pretentious character! Who is he?" Almost no one looks for or listens to a truth that reveals its roots. People prefer ideas that function apart from themselves, that won't make any trouble. Except for a handful of my readers.

One is supposed to be an old man ready to be embalmed. Then people say, "What wisdom!" There's nothing to be afraid of; he's repeating the old story. In order to be heard in France—unless stardom has fallen on you and made what you have to say insignificant—you have to be seventy-five or eighty and shaking all over. Then you're put on exhibit and idolized by the small class of climbers who use the famous to make themselves known. You are lucky not to have become a celebrity, because nothing makes you grow old before your time so much as fame—you begin to take yourself seriously!

In Rome I told myself, "Be serious." I had concocted a solemn and abstract paper; in the cellars of the Vatican you can't be too careful. But at the very moment I got up on the platform, a brief giddiness overcame my good intentions. I tell myself, "It's now or never. There's nothing to lose and nothing to gain; we'll all be dead tomorrow." So I set out to my own music. It goes over; there are a lot of young people in the hall from different seminaries. When the question period begins, a tall man dressed in black, with an ascetic countenance, rises in the middle of the hall.

"Sir, I have only one question to ask you: are you humble?" He stands there alertly, his hands alongside his body. He's someone who has followed me since my childhood, austere and faithful. I feel myself growing smaller, wanting to be an obedient kid again: "Bless me, Father, for I . . . " At the same time an empty space opens up in which anger is gathering. There is a long awkward silence. I tell him as sweetly as I can that answers are contained in questions. For example, if I asked him "Are you an idiot?" he might well think I was making a statement; I should have recognized the humility in his voice. I went on my with regular line—that it's impossible for me to talk about the religious crisis the way people talk about the economic crisis or the problem of the mass media. It was because of my concern for truth that I said "I"; it was not just a question of myself, since there were many others with whom I believed I was in communion. The "I" is deceitful, too; one shouldn't take pride in it, but it creates less illusion. The humility of those who are doctrinaire could be the worst pride, masked and indiscernible.

He remained there, still standing. Pity overwhelmed me. He had stayed on the desert road that I had long followed. He was part of me. I tried to say that I was not talking aggressively, that I was not angry, but serene and friendly. The Church is my mother. But when my mother, whom I loved more than everything, died in her village, a short time later I felt glad. Could he understand?

I hear a weak voice that says, "I hadn't thought about these things. Thank you."

I felt that he was yielding to nostalgia, to the sentimentality about one's mother—that is, to his own death. Catastrophe—tears come to my eyes, the first sounds of sobbing, because of humility probably. Because of my mother. There is a long awkward silence. Shame consumes me.

I've always been slow on the uptake. This is what I would have liked to have said instead of becoming sentimental: Too much reverence kills life. Too many people become suspicious of a thought when it becomes flesh and blood, word. There is also a sin of humility and orthodoxy. Look where virtue has been placed—with the impersonality that people dare to call fidelity. God speaks; the subject disappears. You say that it's enough to forget yourself? Take a closer look at the empty, absent man that you offer us as a model. After all, what is there, apart from us? The *content*, I insist, must first be in human acts, in active love. Formulas are useful, as necessary as the mileage markers along the highways, but they are not the way.

# DOUBT

Science and technology have come to act directly on human thought, thereby revealing and exploiting what is mechanical in it. Of course, in the process they liberate *homo faber* but at the same time they relegate to the museum whatever is linked to intimate experience and is more apt to be expressed obscurely. In many areas cybernetics holds the power to point out the best and only possible choice. But as soon as we enter the moral and spiritual order, technology draws back. Specialists in faith and morality, however, have often acted like computers. It's hardly surprising that their best solutions have succeeded in producing revolt and even indifference.

It's obvious that I have doubts. The days of childhood are over. Bless me, Father, I have doubts. For your penance, say three Hail Marys. Today I believe that absolute conviction entails the most total self-imprisonment, the unpardonable sin, while presenting itself as fidelity. A devilish process that has succeeded in convincing generations that asking questions was wrong. As if doubt wasn't the stimulus at the heart of faith, an endless beginning, in the same way that life is the overcoming of death.

I doubt—that is, my mental consciousness never stops saying no-yes or yes-no, while body-consciousness always moves in one direction and says yes-yes. What seems to move me, what moves the hand that writes this, is to be found more in ignorance than in ideas. Like an energy with its own will.

Someone in love doesn't constantly go around saying "I love you." Love speaks just as well in silence.

My adherence is total. I want everything to be true. Not a day, not an hour rolls by without my thinking, in some way, about eternity. But this bothers me, too. For it's impossible to build anything on it. Criticism never stops. I struggle. Yes, I'm an unbeliever—like you, unless you've yielded to the illusion that the dividing line between faith and disbelief only passes between one person and another and not within each of us. That is why, Your Excellencies, I'm not so happy that you've set up a Secretariat for Non-Believers.

I'm a spy, a double agent, one foot in disbelief. But pay attention: when I say "I," I'm speaking for many.

If someone declares that he's sure of his survival after death and asks me "What about you?" I don't have an answer. Not because I don't believe, but because I don't have the right words to speak of the beyond.

Or if I hear it said that God rewards or punishes, I let it pass. It's outside my concern. If I'm not against a position, that's no reason to think it's all fine; I remain in ignorance with the unexpressed. That's my kind of doubting.

To tell the truth, sometimes my first instinct is to answer, "No, there's no punishment and no survival." That's because there's still a teacher inside me, a need to reduce overconfidence by questioning simplistic formulas.

If people say that the poor need to have a few easy formulas, remember that the poor are the future rich. Let's refuse to allow the poor to be duped by words, even while recognizing that formulas can also lead to communion. But a charity that consists in leaving the "little ones" to their functional religion is a kind of contempt.

But listen, tell us if you believe in the resurrection. Is it a fact, yes or no? No evasion this time.

You want so much for me to reassure you. Like my mother with her little tricks to keep me on her pathways. But when she left, she told me something else, the joyous truth that no one can receive without going through sorrow.

How eager you are for an answer! Either, "Look, he's on our side," or "We told you, he's with the enemy."

I'd prefer not to answer the question put that way because it gives the impression that belief in an historical fact could be the cause of faith; and especially because there are too many ulterior motives and out-of-date ideas that would falsify any response.

I can feel him touching me, all around me. How can you be so blind?

If I happen to speak about God, I prefer to say, "If he exists." Besides, I never speak to anyone of what I love. . . . It seems to me that doubt, introduced in this way, suggests distance, humor, a kind of modesty, a refusal to annex. We don't decide to doubt; it just happens that way. How can I dare to say I believe unless I'm a burning flame, if I don't climb up on the cross? It's fine that you're full of convictions, but recognize that these very convictions mask the indulgence in God to which you abandon yourselves—which is really self-indulgence. To tear down the idols that exist outside oneself doesn't mean much. To destroy idolatry within oneself is far more difficult.

We must allow a word to be uttered, criticize it pitilessly in order to disentangle it from our personal hangups, and ultimately not be certain if we've achieved this. We must accept this poverty while keeping faith in the word, neither glorious nor authoritative, but nevertheless joyful in its active combination of doubt and expectation. Answers are given slowly, but the need for answers is often only a way of indulging in one's anguish. The poet René Char writes, "No bird has the heart to sing in a thicket of questions."

In the area of faith it is both vulgar and stupid to try to prove anything. Fight for truth? Never. People fight for convictions in place of truth. Someone who genuinely loves the truth seeks only to let it fill her whole being.

Don't try to change people's opinions or convert anybody. Be what you are and perhaps someone else will be led to become what she is. Adopt a genuine manner to tell us what moves you, without worrying about the consequences. That's neither laziness nor amateurism, but a spontaneous self-discipline which has nothing in common with a party line. It might better be compared with the constant practice of someone who wants to play in tune.

The path toward faith is also a matter of unlearning things. Spiritual sanity resides in a youthfulness which spontaneously rejects everything that is static. Almighty God, King, Lord, Prosecutor, Judge, Spouse, Lover of the soul, Father—get rid of all those words, and thousands of others, until nothing is left. Nothing, that's our name for God, condemned not to intervene, for fear of making us all immature. That means we shouldn't be afraid to use the most everyday words. Only you know what you've put in them—hidden love, deep laughter.

Be cautious about faith and hope. Skepticism is a better ally than credulity. Despair is more valuable than the superficial assurance that makes hope meaningless.

Remember, God speaks through the lips that happen to be there—those of the unbeliever as well as those of the saint and through the silence of those who no longer have anything to say. Why should you think that there is no longer anything to be learned from certain voices? I've learned as much from "enemies of faith" like Voltaire, Diderot, Feuerbach, Nietzsche and Marx as from Aquinas and his descendants.

In Dostoevsky it's children, drunkards, and the insane who express eternal truths. There are also mystics, who are locked up so that they won't cause trouble.

Don't expect manna every morning, comrades. There's no storehouse, no arsenal of proofs. Instead, there's a sense of being an illegal immigrant, stammering his way through evening courses, with the simple faith of a doubter, feeling like a liar but with the boldness that goes with it, the expectation, some taste for divine joy, along with a secret regret that there are no longer opportunities to get oneself killed for that tiny something, almost nothing, which changes the meaning of everything. And realizing that this is only the imagination, since the fight is right here, obscure but deadly.

I participated last night in a colloquium on the rue de Solferino. Two philosophers spoke. The mechanisms of thought functioned smoothly. It was impressive. Suddenly they got into a disagreement about Lacan. I realized that they belonged to different schools and that, despite the loftiness of their vocabulary, they hadn't yet grown up. Both of them had just had good meals. In the respectful silence which almost always means lack of understanding, rumbling emerged from the bodies of the two debaters and I wondered why everyone didn't burst out laughing. Ah, I said to myself, getting serious again, there's a language that saves them. After we've drawn our last breath, the body continues to speak while emptying itself. Such humility.

Even if faith began to burn brightly, how could it penetrate intimate existence? Ecstasy and miracle would remain foreign to the human substructure and could only build a static world. A universe whose meaning is unique and brilliant would be unbreatheable. You'd immediately become a slave who has only to obey and to imitate, and at the same time you'd be rich with possessions, knowledge, and power. Spiritual life, however, is possible only because of not-knowing. The mentality that presents faith as *natural* betrays it while pretending to serve it. That's why a rigid faith is merely flight from oneself and overcompensation.

And how would I be able to put one foot in front of another, or manage to say a word, if eternity was never absent?

Believers almost always imagine that faith means certitude. It's true enough for the humble, the innocent, the saints, since for them it's a matter of direct perception, interior light. But that's not the human construction we usually call faith. Or rather, it's a certitude composed of suggestions and stoicism—that is, of attachment to self, in the form of faith. So many people speak of hope or love, but they're so pompous—their tone gives them away. Their words are buoys; without them they'd completely collapse. Watch the hands and eyes of those who speak. Learn to recognize the faith that reveals a secret despair.

For me the absence of doubt would be disturbing. Not the kind that suggests flight, laziness, a preoccupation with oneself in the guise of intellectual difficulties. I'm speaking of an active doubt that hunts out prejudices and every kind of idolatry, an ongoing discovery that grows stronger by overcoming all obstacles.

Faith has many wounds, fractures through which one advances and retreats. It cannot be possessed like courage. To hesitate, to change one's mind, to make mistakes, these are proofs of honesty.

Be on guard against certitude, if only because it ignores style. Once we are so installed in a conviction that it seems to be natural, we're no longer interested in how it's expressed. We prefer to think that it all takes place in our head. That's nonsense.

Your certitudes—are you so blind? What are they generally based on? The failure to deepen your knowledge. We rush past questions in order to avoid anxiety.

At the same time, it's true that taking refuge in obscurity can be a cop-out. When I refer to the unknown or to non-knowledge, I'm not thinking of people who want, at little cost to themselves, to avoid the process of learning. Yes, forgetting is necessary, but in order to forget one first must know. I'd be very suspicious of someone who went in for abstract painting before knowing how to sketch a tree or a pitcher.

One cannot decide to learn how to doubt; it happens unexpectedly, opening up unsuspected, murmuring avenues of approach. It goes along with a fear of illusion, which is a kind of love; it gets us started.

The doubter is as hard on his or her own doubt as on credulity. Such a person keeps on going to the very end of doubt, out of an indefectible faith. To live may also involve losing your faith and coming to realize that you are "possessed" by it.

Doubt creates a joyous game, the constant astonishment that's at the heart of language. A wound of separation. Every word is a cry: "My God, why have you abandoned me?"

Every image that we accept once and for all hinders communion. By his absence-presence Jesus is more present than in the flesh. Every spiritual experience, if it's not just imaginary, is rooted in this understanding. For there are hosts of experiences that are only the prejudices of reason, the products of strange ideas.

That's why to meet God is at the same instant to deny him. Every certitude is a way of "putting God to death." Classical atheism has its roots in certitudes. Fanatical certitudes and negations are related.

Some weep for the certitudes of the past. We must preserve, they say, this or that which was beautiful and good. Perhaps that's true, but those who complain like that are weeping for themselves. In the last analysis, we shouldn't weep but create. Gothic churches were built over Romanesque structures, which were built over pagan fountains and temples. To create is the only important thing, to rediscover the fervor that produced the thing you're weeping for. Conservatives never go back far enough. Progressives dream too much of the future. A true revolution always rediscovers the source of a tradition and expresses it in body and soul at the same instant.

In your eyes, both when I reread the Gospel and when I compare it with what it's become in so many minds, I'm using what you call "the archaic language of childhood." Are you so sure? How confident you are about placing the word of Abraham and the anti-Abrahamic word in opposition. How quick you are to point out those who remain prisoners of myths and folklore. But in order to be unrooted it's first necessary to be rooted. I suspect you didn't carry away with you the beating of the earth's heart, the "poem" which makes every disciple an exile, a foreigner, a citizen of the third or fourth world, even when he plays a role in the marvelous circus of modern life. My modest hope is that the word of childhood with its outworn poetry, when it's carried within oneself like a wound that has been cured of nostalgia, because of its close ties with the word of the Gospel, is more revolutionary than your ideological structures. Nothing is more revolutionary than childhood.

I was about to make a fool of myself. I'm not prejudiced in favor of childhood; a whole lifetime is needed to conquer it. Nothing is more dangerous than to believe that one possesses a monopoly on childhood. Fortunately, it doesn't take long to become senile.

# IDEOLOGY

Short trip to black Africa. In the large cities bureaucrats and intel-lectuals are more Westernized than their European counterparts. A few kilometers away, however, those villages with wells resemble our traditional villages. Nostalgia once more overcomes me.

Nevertheless, in both countryside and city, priests who have been converted to audiovisual techniques dispense religious instruction. Rejection of the faith is more rapid than it was in Europe. "Atheism," one of them tells me, citing Dostoevsky, "is the last stage before per-fect faith. In some areas Christian colonialism helped establish a whole moral order; from the womb of this Christianity mystical re-volutionaries are emerging." I can't help noticing that the speaker has come to accept the dialectic of history, but is the Gospel directly involved in history?

One can justify everything. Dialectic, too, can offer consolation and help us to sleep peacefully. But how can it mask illusion? The Christian prejudice, in the West as everywhere else, has been to *in-struct*—that is, to cram things in, as if filling a hole, in the manner of national educational examiners, instead of *e-ducate*, to help some-thing grow, to give birth to new life, to encourage the inner person. Genuine education implies a process of stripping away, forgetting es-tablished mental categories and having confidence in a word that speaks through every race and ends up joining with the Word.

I would so like to believe that the "childhood" of Christendom is over, that it is breaking away from ideology and legalism, no longer emphasizing concepts—the Western representation of things—tear-ing down its doctrinal scaffolding, or at least keeping it at a distance, something for specialists, and becoming at once more feeble and more strong, more apt to express itself in terms of our common an-thropological foundation. Deprived of its regionalistic condition-ing—of that tiny region called Europe—Christianity might be more capable of worldwide diffusion, without any idea of conquest.

But when I talk like this, I, too, am giving in to general ideas. I'd so much like to believe that the white race in a decline that one can clearly observe in population graphs and in world events, in new laws which merely ape new customs—which may be good but are also clear signs of decadence—I'd like to believe that the whites are not going to bring about the destruction of Christian faith along with their own collapse.

What an odd way to talk! The white race was not given the prom-ise of eternal life. I know very well that there will always be conflict between those who identify faith with a culture and those who are receptive to the power of the leaven at the very moment that faith seems reduced to nothing.

The alienated disciple, wandering without knowing any longer where to turn, may always discover that it wasn't faith but ideology that was doing his thinking.

In analyzing the religious phenomenon, Feuerbach and Marx—although it would be necessary to add nuances in regard to Marx's position—had simply taken the social data into account but, fascinated by the discovery of alienation, had ignored a key fact that has become obvious today.

Let's push their position to the extreme and assume that faith is simply the product of historical situations. But this product, whatever its source, can modify the conditions that produced it. Experience shows that mystical or prophetic movements, whether they underlie religion or are produced by it, have the power to relativize existing society and challenge religion itself to the degree that it is at the service of that society. Materialism has merely been able to point out only that religious faith in its static form concealed a ferment of liberation. Before the infinity of God, all doctrines and institutions reveal their contingency. As throughout the Bible, the prophets are those who never leave existing structures intact. They can at first seem to be primarily destructive, but they create an uneasiness that allows for a new birth.

The prophet receives the Gospel not as knowledge but as a word for the present instant, implying both commitment and criticism. That's how one unmasks bad faith, which attempts to make eternal what is only temporary. It's also how intellectual positions are relativized and institutions are seen as human creations. By cutting through the network of religious ideas that have in part become prejudices protecting the present social order as the only reasonable and possible one, the prophet provokes upheaval.

It then becomes evident that faith does not tolerate injustice, that God is not on the side of legal justice or envy but demands interior justice. Prayer can no longer nourish fantasy or veil reality. In this way the Gospel, read by the prophet in communion with the Church and against that within the Church which resists life and the Spirit, will rouse us from a religion of sloth that seemed to guarantee our relationship to God while leaving us absent to our neighbor.

A religion can be exported as an aspect of colonialist pressure but still give birth to freedom and love. Numerous examples in quite a few countries around the world reveal this paradox today. Genuine disciples are scattered here and there in prison, are tortured, even killed, along with others who have no hope beyond the human. Of course, there is a constant risk of identifying this new faith with a new political order. Our spiritual struggle never ends. No one knows from what direction the Spirit will emerge.

The kingdom is like leaven which, after all, is decaying substance. That's the side you should be on. The kingdom is not proclaimed only by and on behalf of the poor, but also by dubious controversial types. When faith becomes what it is, interior liberation, it is spontaneously creative. The Gospel is corrosive; had you forgotten?

At the very moment you don't expect it, just when you thought you were in agreement, comes a piece of foolishness: "But I tell you, love your enemies." Or he advises you to make friends of the mammon of iniquity. . . . He breaks the circle in which we've parcelled out our desires and then disappears, leaving us adrift. It's impossible to make him an idol. He offers no other law or justification than the Father's, whose justice is not ours, whose love is beyond reason.

The empty tomb, the ascension, remember, mean Jesus Christ become Word, the Holy Spirit who drags us on to a paradoxical fulfillment.

By looking on Jesus as a free person I am able to make myself his ally, because he is on the side of the poor and the weak, and against the multinationals and the oil companies and the coffee lobby—that is, against everything that keeps men and women from being neighbors, from becoming close to each other in the present moment.

Nevertheless, it's impossible to imagine that he looks on the world as a structure to improve, a work to complete, or that he wants to busy himself, as we do, building a world on nothingness in order to conceal its emptiness with science, history, and progress. In one sense our planet has been handed over to its own counsel, a gigantic, interlocking network of relationships, almost physically determined. The kingdom is for here and now, in the heart of the human. If it creates love and joy, that's a bonus, so to speak. The Gospel is the grain of sand which disrupts the machine, the break in the wall of necessity. As soon as it wants to create its own sphere, it collapses.

The absence of Jesus is the sign of God's love. It prevents any of our cherished schemes from becoming finally installed. The world is caught up in the wake of the impossible—which is also the necessary.

There's no need to go to Africa to "understand" Africa. In Paris, as everywhere, the Africans regroup in tribes and rebuild their villages—this time in cement. For them there are no orphans, no marginal people, no one is excluded—except the barren wife. To think of them as unhappy is a Western idea—unhappiness is simply part of life. There they are—poor, close to each other, peace in their eyes, with a joy we have lost.

A telegram arrives: Drame Dramane learns that his young wife has died. A telephone call to the office to say that he will be out for a day to receive condolences. But this mourning has nothing in common with ours. The men and women who arrive say, "Pôle, pôle," a Swahili word full of sweetness, like touching someone's face with your hand. They sit down on the ground; the women chant; the men remain quiet. Death is natural.

Dusseynou has been sick. Three months' convalescence in the countryside. But he has no money for the trip. No need to worry. The "brothers" get involved instantly; the necessary sum is collected. Dusseynou will return in three months; he will have lost his job. A few days before his return, they will take up another collection.

Few wives remain here with their husbands very long. Often married by proxy, they come so that they can have a child, and then leave. For an African woman it is the child that counts; the husband isn't very important. That's why the wives of a polygamous husband generally get along well, sharing all their tasks.

The Africans who organize rent strikes or join demonstrations are usually students who have already been Westernized. They're full of words like imperialism, capitalism, and alienation. The ordinary workers are outside of all that, or beyond it; sometimes they imitate the students, usually without conviction. These people are nobles. Where do they get their peace, their equanimity regarding tomorrow? One would almost say that fraternity is natural to them. How strange to talk about bringing them the Gospel—they're living it.


No. We must make a break with nostalgia. The Gospel enlightens our human condition. It drags the individual from the clan, from the family, from one's childhood. It makes everyone solitary, a wanderer, a marginal being. It is up to each of us to recreate a communion, but now with the awareness of individual freedom. There is always a desert to cross.

The societies of the West have not succeeded in rebuilding effective solidarity. Or you have to believe, with Michelet, that there was a brief period in the high Middle Ages when millions of people lived in a world that opened onto hope. So much so that in the midst and in spite of wars, famines, and plagues, something like joy reigned. Perhaps. The ideologues of our time also try to recreate a commu-

130

nion but they only offer various hopes. Each wishing to be all, they separate as much as they unite and provide no joy.

## Action Is Born of a Fundamental Discovery

There's no point in attacking ideology itself, which is a short or long-term plan expressed in a body of doctrine, on which concrete action is based and judged. Ideology's aim, therefore, exists apart from consciences, allowing individuals to avoid their endless quest.

What would be more natural in economics and politics? How would modern societies be able to survive otherwise? By permitting men and women to be thought of and located in determined conditions, it organizes their energies and orients them with a view to coherence and efficiency. In this way the crowd is carried along without knowing it. In a world that is prey to unrestrained competition, which is a kind of war, the advantages are obvious—but so are the dangers. For sooner or later it can appear that ideologies are ultimately only the crystallization of situations, desires, and justifications that are given the name of science, rationality, or faith.

Ideology, precisely because it lends individuals powerful support, tends to substitute itself for them and to crush individual consciences because they are dangerous. Creative liberty is eliminated to the profit of what is mechanical and stagnant. Only a constant state of alert can prevent petrification: that's where the Gospel comes in.

Ideologies are given fantastic support by the latest technology. In many areas computers allow us to find solutions and eliminate hesitation and uncertainty. This represents considerable progress, at least in principle, since human intelligence is thereby freed for its true task, which is creative. At the same time, however, in its fascination with the machine, human thought reveals more and more of its inherently mechanical tendency. Polarized by the concern for indefinite development and short-term profitability, it tends to function in a closed system.

The fact that biologists are able to consider transcribing the codes of nucleic acids into the human genetic formula is extremely significant. In this way several shortcuts could be taken. By incorporating certain aptitudes in the nucleus of the egg—speaking, walking, singing, painting, etc.—they would immediately have a complete person, available for human tasks.

Such absurdity allows us to better understand the fundamental evil of the ideologies of Progress. Whether they admit it or not, the purpose of modern societies, capitalist or socialist, is to produce human beings. We look with horror at certain designated countries where doctrine is communicated by loudspeakers at every street corner. But we don't always see that in a more subtle manner we are submitted to the same treatment. The distance between the individual and the social is constantly shrinking. What is important is fitting into a pattern. The model finally imposes its desires and its approach on everyone, telling us how we should act, live, and die. And those who protest against the proposed model are also being conditioned. Technological organization, though claiming to exist for the happiness of others, has become the ultimate purpose of things.

The result is that societies which believe themselves liberated from taboos, sin and hell are surrounded by rules and iron railings, a prey to solitide and fear. For when God is repressed, violence is less apt to be offset by love. A police regime follows.

The Gospel has something essential to say to such a world. Lilies of the field are able to shoot up among the computers and birds of the air can perch on them. Of itself, faith is creative and places the individual at a distance from social conformity and ideology. It can be seen once more as what it really is—a force for liberation, not simply rejecting ideologies but pointing out their secret vice.

This presumes that faith has not itself become, to a great degree, an ideology. If it wants to communicate with our disintegrating modern societies, it is forced to reduce itself to essentials.

Charles Wackenheim's *Christianity Without Ideology* frankly pointed out that in its cultural expression faith has often become an ideology, quite naturally, so to speak, in the inner workings of the Church. Undoubtedly he has overstated his thesis—it's the nature of the genre—giving the impression that a Christianity without ideology is able to exist, but his analysis is extremely rich.

The natural tendency of every doctrinal system is to reduce the praxis of living men and women to nothing more than an epiphenomenon and end up with an exclusively institutional definition of Christianity. Instead of an approach that proceeds from experience to truth, the emphasis is on ideas to be incarnated. Instead of going from the concrete to the abstract, it goes from the abstract to the concrete. It thus tends to concentrate on a particular area, and to communicate theories about man and the world, whereas Christianity is above all a form of human conduct that has been activated by a prophetic utopia in the midst of civil societies.

Religious ideology is faith that has been degraded into "religion." Of course it is pointless to want to separate faith and religion in concrete experience, but we can see very well how ossification is produced. Fear of the future and of one's own uniqueness, fear of a love that would demand unselfishness, a preference for legalistic agreements that create an aura of security—these are the eternal roots of "religion." They veil the contradictions and shortcomings of experience with the help of a ready-made supernatural order, which provides automatic answers, making critical reflection superfluous.

Such a "religion" puts God at the service of our needs. It is invaluable for a while since it can provide security and inner strength, unifying our ego, suppressing our uncertainties and offering hope and firm convictions. But it refuses to recognize to what extent it is a human product over which we have power, until a form of voluntary deprivation takes place and a bold faith comes to the fore. I have seen this happen, most often among older people, sometimes at death's door. Such faith does not reject religion but keeps it at a distance.

Doctrinal construction tends to place faith's center of gravity in the past. Everything happens as if knowledge and obedience were the beginning of what faith is aiming at. This makes it almost impossible to discover that something else is at stake. But I don't want to oversimplify. In spite of cultural pressures the faith-that-is-love sometimes shows itself stronger and expresses itself despite overly fixed forms. When I moved in Catholic circles I met many men and women of a rare purity and love, which was often disguised by the vocabulary and reflex-reactions they had inherited. I felt both admiration and pity to see how they lived and spoke behind sheets of plate glass.

The Bible is perfectly clear on this. After Ezekiel, the loving tenderness of Amos and Hosea serve to dissolve all formalism. The Gospels contrast ritual to the love of God and neighbor, which sums up the law (Jn 5:6; Mk 2:27; Mt 12:8; Lk 6:9). It's quite clear; mystics and saints of every century, as well as countless ordinary people, have lived in that light.

It's impossible to quibble about this. The object of faith, we repeat, is neither a catalogue of truths, nor even truth; it is to love God in knowing his love for us, even if this love has little in common with what we imagine love to be. As a result, Christian love consists in loving others, not in words and ideas, but in acts (Jn 3:19). It calls for the creation here and now of a new relationship with others.

All through history unnecessary shoots have sprouted up, additional canonical and liturgical rules that have petrified our relationship with God and our neighbor. Then follows the progressive disappearance of creative freedom; the pedagogy of prayer is hardened into a rule book. The Lateran Council and the Council of Trent made the paschal encounter a legal obligation with penalties. Faith, torn apart in divided churches, organized the struggle against rationalism that existed outside itself without always noticing the same virus within.

The time has come for Christianity to resolutely leave the world of fear and war, which is more or less the natural and necessary world of materialist ideologies; otherwise, it will be only one ideology among others. Not that it must systematically reject the orderly presentation of doctrine. Each generation expresses its spiritual vision of the world and creates its own plan of the Church. How could it be otherwise without surrendering to utopia? What is important is to accept everything that is not essential to the message as provisional and contingent and to struggle for a greater transparency. For nothing is worse than to abandon concrete existence for social or even moral ends, allowing oneself to believe that in the spiritual order action is born from doctrine. Action is born from an interior experience, in the communion of faith, which is itself a creative diversity.


### For Those Who Really Want To Know

Today's "religious crisis" is real only for those minds that have been captured by ideology—that is, those who have adopted some preconceived representation of human life and faith. Such is the illusion that avoids hearing the naked word. It encourages people to fool themselves with dreams about an earlier period of faith or of one that is about to come, "the post-crisis," according to the wonderful formula used by some American bishops, who learned it from industrial leaders. In this way many are able once again to repress reality. So many men find an unavowed pleasure in debates, unrelated to any genuine commitment. Few are ready to pay the price of tension, suspicion, and solitude. Nevertheless, the Christian communion is made up of traditions, ruptures, fidelity, anger, love and joy. . . .

There is a crisis only because men and women were coerced—that is, subjected to ideas. Doctrine pretended to guide them, skipping the stage of fundamental experience, or called "encounter" what had little in common with one. As Jean Delumeau reminds us, "Voltaire received Communion more often than Pascal."

Perhaps Jung is right. The Church proposed to humanity an ideal that was unrooted in experience, and was therefore impossible to achieve. The whole of modern progress has been driven into the gulf that was created in consciences by the sense of the impossible and its ensuing guilt. Powerful ideologies have put the passion for the absolute at the service of unlimited growth, domination, comfort and pleasure. In this way Christendom has been not only directly but indirectly the creator of history.

The idea that humanity represents merely degradation and deserves contempt, which is popular among some of the most celebrated minds of our time, could only flourish in the West. How could someone today who is both clearsighted and without faith, cut off from the body of life, incapable of being fooled by the mirage of happiness, how could such a person not feel absurd?

To believe that the world is on the march to its fulfillment can only provoke mockery. In the face of the nuclear arms buildup, the growth of world population and the pathetic hopes offered by publicity experts, only a comic response makes sense. Hope must come from elsewhere—from the heart of the earth and the depth of heaven.

Some complain of decadence, others see a new springtime—that's really ideology speaking. It's here and now that we must love, play, laugh, and risk our lives.

If I say that this world is beautiful and good, that I love it, this doesn't mean that I'm not aware of the horror, the degradation, and the danger of impending catastrophe. I'm speaking of what is true in consciences that are stronger than evil.

To create a joyous world in this very instant, out of the misery and happiness that is offered—that, too, is the human vocation, provided that we refuse to leave the world as it is. But the person who dwells in her truth transforms the earth. In reality, what may be only flight, evasion, and nostalgia in one individual can be experience and action for another.

Christian language, as soon as it moves away from experience and is no longer verified by it, becomes elastic, full of distortions and quibbles, concerned with syntheses and false harmony. When we embroider emptiness with abstract formulas, we have the very opposite of a language of hope.

A piece of quartz is as spiritual as one of Pascal's *Pensees*, Maeterlinck wrote. The fundamental sin is not to live one's life fully but to identify it with mental representations. Detachment from sensuality is essential but has nothing in common with escape into idealism. One cannot tame love and make it obligatory for the greater good of others. There is no such thing exactly as Christian morality. Of course, faith immediately implies a morality in the sense of an action dictated by love, but precisely because of this it does not express itself within a particular moral system. Its ultimate creative purpose cuts through all established moralities.

The truth is that atheists and agnostics are the most faithful defenders of a static and functional religion. They need to envisage a knowledge fixed in immutable forms, linked to a purely social ethics, which can thereby be kept at a distance.

That is what is atheistic about so many believers who resist the movement of spiritual liberation. They speak of tradition but they don't go back far enough.

The faith that society easily accepts is one that can be located among other ideologies, perfectly immersed in history, even though it may itself be a witness for transcendence. Such a faith goes along with the game of appearances, and shows up regularly on TV talk shows.

"Let's not kid each other," people say sarcastically. "If the Gospel really penetrated the consciences of individuals and took over a society, life would become impossible. Let's face it—the Gospel isn't directly concerned with the human species or the family or money or progress."

Well, there's nothing to worry about. The Gospel only reaches a small number at any depth—although, without them, the majority would be corrupted. You know it as well as I do. The others, whether Christians or not, play the lottery, watch football, buy, sell, fornicate. A small number; that's the way it is. For whoever, neither better nor worse than others perhaps, genuinely fulfills the Gospel is in one way or another excluded and condemned. The world has to resist love in order to endure; it's necessary, in the order of things. So don't be afraid of those who struggle against ideology and law. Leave them to their utopia, their happiness.

Just as a neurotic who becomes aware during analysis of the roots of his agony is terribly afraid of being freed of it, in the same way many believers exist only in and by means of crisis. Whether they take a stand against novelty or criticize everything as old-fashioned, they use up all their energy in blame and praise. But what if the crisis were resolved? It would then be necessary for them to live the values of contemplation and love. It's not certain they really want to. Or I, unfortunately.

136

Why do you think it's necessary to be poor in order to achieve inner change? Must one live in a slum? What's the highest salary at which it's possible to encounter God? This is all ideological twaddle. Genuine illumination makes one poor instantly; having loses its importance. Greed is also capable of filling the hearts of the poor who are rich with all they do not yet possess. What's important is to be open to what takes place, for "Poverty is a great illumination/coming from within."

In this world controlled by money it's hardly possible for anyone to be poor today in the manner of Francis of Assisi. They'd become part of folklore and be immediately taken over by the media. Anyway, it's pointless to imitate the actions of the poor; poverty has to be a new creation, coming to birth in the depths of the soul. To step forward without anxiety at the high noon of death, in the midst of every human passion. To accept the world joyously without being duped by its values.

The encounter with God is the supreme sign of wealth. It's better to set out along the road to cover the distance that separates us from him. And if there's only an abyss under our feet, to cry out or keep silent. To invite someone to renunciation when the sacrifice is not directed at the good of the other person is to make oneself the accomplice of a deception. God has no need of sacrifices; men and women do.

One day a writer met me on the sidewalk and told me, "You keep preaching love because we have to live together, right? Not everybody is lucky enough to escape. You make love the way to social harmony; that kind of love disgusts me."

Don't think that the anti-Christianity of our time, which is far more dangerous than you think because it's rarely allowed to speak openly, distinguishes between Christians who believe this or that. They attack the Christian idea as revealed in the attitudes around them. It's an idea with little grandeur, easily demolished, because it's made in the image of society. Tell unbelievers that their atheism will lead to suicide and they'll laugh in your face. I don't mind being lumped together with the mass of Christians and feel myself in solidarity with them, but that's no reason not to struggle against false conceptions of love.

There is a sacrificial love that is a personal act, and an exploitative love that expresses an ugly individualism—that's the difference between agape and eros. How can we rid ourselves of the dangerous ideal that leads us to pursue the phantom of what ought to be instead of being present to what is, making us fugitives from reality? Saying "Do not do unto others," relying on prohibitions and taboos—all that is completely pointless as long as the link between myself and others has not been perceived. Instead, say "Don't harm yourself." Spare me your love, especially if it's sacrificial. Don't bind me with your ties of honey; I can't stand that kind of humility. I prefer a dangerous love, a love that hurts. Perhaps a wild flower will grow within it, as pure as a diamond.

Don't tell me any more about your love for humanity; that's only your drug.

One does not love out of duty.

One does not love in the past or in the future.

Love is new or it is unreal.

Beyond security.

Certainly, we're asked to complete the unity which is the sign of Jesus (Jn 13:34). Yes, this was given us as a commandment, but from within love. We are never asked to substitute words and ideas for the reality of love.

From need to desire, from desire to love, from love to self-forgetfulness.

Love begins by laying waste, and opens onto the absolute, even if few people perceive it. Impossible to hold it captive. It happens unexpectedly, then creates its own necessity and its armed wisdom.

If we think of love as simply the play of desire, of pleasure and habit, if there's no detachment—that is, if sovereign death is not in some way both present and absent within the instant—there is no joy.

Desire reaches out beyond itself. To sin is to deliberately halt along the way and reject the joy of self-liberation.

What are we to do in the midst of our tangled lives? Nothing, except to let love act. To become its accomplice, in happiness or sorrow. To put oneself second. To love without hope of return. Every pain can become a lasting joy, starting today.


## The Honor of Being Human

It's embarrassing to hear someone say that he's praying, that he's been praying or is about to pray. Do you talk like that about love? There's no hope for someone like that. Of course, he might be a saint; language is deceptive.

How refreshing are those people who never pray, who don't have

138

words for everything, who seem rather to repress prayer. Their silence sometimes speaks for them.

To pray is to set out, to love, to write, to paint, and to die at each instant.

A person who asks if it's necessary to pray today makes it clear that she's still speaking from within the framework of ideology. We don't *have to:* prayer rises up from the heart of life.

But prayer can also become a terrible weight and be abandoned; then one day it begins to invade one's existence. We don't decide— it happens or doesn't happen. "Prayer is not perfect," Cassien says, "if the one who prays is aware of himself and realizes that he is praying."

Prayer is often auto-suggestion, set in motion by words. We need to make use of words against words, to unmask complacency and dishonesty, and to realize that we often try to use God as a tool. Praying is a struggle. It's a matter of going beyond faith in one's own thoughts in order to rediscover the original faith. Business executives are imprisoned in their steel or glass towers, but those dedicated to the interior life and religious ideas can just as easily be walled up inside their cloisters. Let's not have too much reverence for the interior life; it's a production like any other until a breakthrough takes place, which is prayed for and expressed in action. We can then speak of a certain greatness of soul whereby a person becomes a partner in God's creation.

Naturally, God's doesn't need prayers. Let's stop turning him into a potentate anxious for homage. It's you and I who need prayer so that we will no longer be alone, in order to get out of our shells and rejoin the universal body of love. We can't link up with others without passing through what is furthest away; to get there it's necessary to lose one's identity. It's in that loss that I can find you, that you can find yourself. To pray is therefore to introduce love, humor, and death into every action and ideology. Hence prayer is the revolutionary act *par excellence,* the very opposite of alienation.

To count sheep or the cracks in the sidewalk, to surrender to habit in order to feel we've settled accounts with ourselves and with God— why not? It can happen that the most wretched prayer is lifted up by love, to the confusion of all hypocrites. But the person who wants to hold back, to keep everything locked up, secretly refusing the flux of time and death, is only pretending. It's the same as multiplying formal gestures of courtesy when love departs. Politeness is the surest way of keeping one's distance.

To pray is to confess. Confess what? That we are empty, that we are hungry. We all use our mouths to eat and to cry out. A vital necessity, prayer is an act of poverty. Damnation implies privation. Those who do not pray damn themselves—that is, they remain *deprived*, shut up in their private property.

Malraux writes that "Art highlights the honor of being human." The honor of whom, of what? The Legion of Honor to be placed on our coffins? And Nietzsche says: "It is shameful to pray." While art may be a sign and a promise, for the disciple art is only a dream and a lie. To the words of Malraux and Nietzsche the believer responds that honor does not consist in the survival of the work of art which does not have the time to see the stars go out, nor in "the dialogue of forms through the millennia," nor in the rejection of humility; all that is only wretchedness, distraction, and self-complacency. Honor means opening oneself to the transcendence that every work of art implies. It is to struggle against the closed universe, the pretensions of every geographical area, and all doctrinal, ideological or aesthetic frameworks—which we easily turn into fortresses. "Modern man," who is so degraded that he no longer takes pleasure in the tragic vision of his destiny, but yields to the indifference of the herd on the way to the slaughterhouse, should remember that prayer, like death, far from being a humiliation, bears witness that we can only attain our full human stature by opening ourselves to the absolute.

## You Are the Meaning and the Way

Who would still dare to talk seriously about Providence? It's a subject that has been too often used to cover up holes, like destiny, fate, and chance, fanning the air in order to say nothing. To speak in the name of God, to pretend to know his ways, both in daily life and history, is to surrender to ideology.

That's what gave rise to those clever theories about evil that helped to anaesthetize entire generations. Soon they began to explain evil as a necessary means of achieving good, and then as the necessary counterpart of the good. A fine conjuring trick, which conceded that God was restrained by logical necessity. Or that God wanted to limit himself in order to leave us free, as if the only way he could arrange things was so that people wouldn't freely choose the good. Within a particular cultural circle such ideas were seen as unquestionable. The important thing is to arrange everything so that it all fits perfectly into a mental system. In this way faith becomes a super-reason which pretends to attain its object.

Such, at least in some mentalities, is the theology of evasion that believed itself absolutely established. But it's impossible today to think or to express oneself within the vocabulary established by such academicism, whether old or new. Its very approach can only be felt as false. A genuine word is born out of its anthropological roots, within the womb of a spiritual experience. One does not capture truth; it leaves only its feathers behind in our descriptions.

For a long time language was able to model the intention and thought of its users and give direction to their feelings. But one day people perceived that its confidence was misplaced. It's impossible to turn back.

Some continue to surrender to principles and interpretations out of a need for security; the social environment is still powerful or they say to themselves that what already exists is better than what is to come. Others, out of neurotic attachment, over-compensate frenetically and think themselves faithful. "They love God," Eckhart says, "the way a peasant loves his cow, for the butter and cheese it produces." But there are also those for whom I write, who are no longer either for or against, but elsewhere, who have entered into the great silence. As in the motto I saw painted on some trucks: "I roll for you."

In itself faith doesn't provide any explicit theory about the world. The Gospel isn't concerned to know why men and women were created; catechism is. All that is rational and useful, but not much fun. This God who created Adam in order to be glorified bores me. There are too many people preoccupied with what it all means; let's get going. You are the meaning and the way.

Life bears its reasons within itself. When it looks for them in ideas, it's a sign of weakness. So many people today no longer listen to the Word, and hence can't go out to meet it, because they're in poor health. They're preoccupied with the meaning of life instead of living in a way that would give it meaning.

Interpretation, however perfect, doesn't exist once and for all. Or else nothing has been learned about the coming and going of words. Try using mummies to express something that's alive.

Any formulation is like an optical instrument, which is not made to be observed or idolized. It does not contain but aims at a reality that is further away. "The act of belief does not terminate in what can be expressed," Aquinas says, "but in the thing itself." Optics has made some progress. We perhaps know a little better these days what language is, how we are born swaddled up in it, that we must achieve our own identity through it, with it or against it, in order to create something new. Every formulation inevitably tends to substitute itself for experience, just as faith tends to be nothing more than a social passport. To think that an official creed would help us achieve Christian unity reflects a certain blindness. One person more or less in the Trinity would hardly worry a large number of sincere believers. Behind the phrases we use, within our attitudes, there's a whole world of bric-a-brac that would be worth examining. The truth is that when someone sets out on the road it's never in the name of an abstract idea. Ultimately, there's only one path; to take another is merely to wander. But the voyager is the only one who knows it. Set out from where you are; otherwise, you'll never arrive anywhere. Nothing takes place without communion, but no communion ever dispenses us from being true to ourselves.

I see your face; I hear your voice behind the windowpane of writing. "After a few generations have experienced a Christianity without ideology, what will be left?" you ask.

There's no utopia. Formulation is a necessary stage; ideology is undoubtedly inevitable. Who would not veil his face before the burning bush? What is new is the boldness, the constant concern to aspire to transparency, the ardor to create and destroy in order to recreate, so as to better adhere to the interior Word that exists within the body of humanity.

The Christian community will survive, more dispersed, no longer preoccupied about making history through mass action, but inscribed within it, preventing history from becoming enclosed within itself. Such a Christianity would be present within ideologies like a yeast or an explosive. Expelled from numerous territories which it had developed, invited to a spontaneous exodus, more concentrated on its own secret, Christianity would more easily permit an evangelical meaning to appear, a new creation that would be more able to grow in all territories without any sense of colonialism. Its losses would be gains.

Some theologians already exist, torn between two worlds, pursuing a solitary way on behalf of a deeper communion, sometimes under attack, more prophetic than doctrinaire. They too roll for you.

Marcel Jousse was a great scholar—anthropologist, linguist, exegete, deliberately interdisciplinary—and prophet of the death of Christian ideology. For a long time he was almost unknown. Quite a few well-known experts borrowed from his work without acknowledging it. That's the nature of things; it's hard to struggle against the tide. Teilhard, also a Jesuit, had all the luck. A scholar, but of a more literary bent, he yielded to the vertigo of the all-inclusive theory, extrapolated lyrically, and thereby rallied intellectuals who were seeking a vision of the world.

Bultmann gained renown in much the same way. You recall that in *Kerygma and Myth,* in order to make the faith accessible to the modern world, he tries to disassociate it from the myths in which it is expressed. For him the cosmology of the Gospel is obsolete and only raises unnecessary questions. What does it mean to say "He descended into hell, ascended into heaven, and sits at the right hand of the Father"? Once again a talented theologian has allowed himself to be overly influenced by philosophy. In wanting to translate the Gospel into the existential language of Heidegger, Bultmann conveyed the feeling that it was radically impossible to evoke God with what is not God. But after it has been demythologized and dehistoricized, the only thing faith can do is breed itself, thereby becoming its own object.

Jousse's approach is almost the opposite of Bultmann's. Mythical language underlines the central theme of faith: the Word is made flesh, God has become earthly, "objective," this-worldly, datable. Why be astonished when we hear that the sun rises or sets, or when people speak of the foot of the mountain, its breasts, its teeth, or its head? Words are spontaneously emptied of their original meaning. An excessive love of absolute abstraction only indicates a spiritual impotence.

Bultmann remains a man of concepts and philosophy, foreign to the word-poem of the Gospel, while Jousse is both anthropologist and poet. It's not images that get in the way of reality but sickly people who are uprooted or perhaps never had roots, and who have lost contact with what lies beyond the tangible. It's not an obsolete folk-religion that Jousse sees in the Gospel but the eternal common foundation of humanity.

Haunted by the traumas that schools create, Jousse experimented, and noticed what so many others say simply out of habit. Shriveled children, hands clutching their pen-handles. "The most ignoble conquest of man is man." Fine lad, but our job is to break him in, to teach him to grab, possess, and fight. Yes, a student rebels when the hours of instruction and study are prolonged, when in the absence of responsibilities he can see the truth of society. But sooner or later he has to return home, get on the right road to raise his standard of living, unless he's willing to become a permanent dropout. That's how Jousse saw the clever little monkey on whom society imposed the slogans of the tribe in order to channel his creative needs into profitable labors.

Jousse was upset by what he heard in pulpits or in courses offered by priest-scholars. They hold forth, provide elaborate proofs, and destroy what is life and poetry in order not to have to apply it to reality.

Jousse saw the so-called "primitive" straining toward and absorbing everything in an absolutely unique manner, internalizing things into his vision and work, transposing them vocally in a spontaneous abstraction, a subjective assimilation, giving intelligence to life, recording the real before a term is used for it, repeating the movement in his own rhythm—that's what Jousse called the primordial anthropological basis of things. Culture is only a polish, the culture of those who repress their individual savagery, separate us from others and from God, kill life, and block action, the very thing that matters in the Gospel.

And what about artists or writers? Because they have insufficiently shed the child within the adult, they try to rediscover the original impact of things by going beyond the dead text to connect up again with living gestures. They make use of words while exorcising them; they rid them of sedimentation, and turn them against themselves in order to break convention. In spite of the pressures of habit and mental laziness they give expression to a unique encounter. Their writing is simultaneously word. In such writing individual words have flesh, a face of their own; they tremble with every movement of the body. To be read is to be eaten. The best reader is the one who transforms the work totally into herself, enjoying her own music.

In the spiritual order there are no professors, only discoverers who reveal to others while they gradually renew themselves. They're the ones whom we try to re-enact within ourselves, who start us on our way without even wanting to. They hold no worldly authority; their only authority is that of *authors*—that is, those who engender, nourish and increase life. Not people who know how to manipulate others. There is a written kind of thinking that is a pure fabrication of the intelligence, a pious discourse that only produces death; it's born of suggestion, fear, the purely mental—of everything that does not emerge from action and experience. A person knows and is moved only by what she receives within herself in obscurity and re-enacts spontaneously. Meaning does not exist first in syllables and phrases, but makes its way through flesh itself.

Greece falsified everything. "When I find myself faced with a difficulty in translating," Jousse writes, "instead of doing what is usually done, taking the Greek term and going through all the literature of the Greco-Latin world which constantly distorts the problems for us, I do the opposite: I go to the Aramaic, taking the viewpoint of anthropology, no longer concerned about whether or not the Greeks existed."

The Gospels are born in a Palestinian and semitic universe. That's where I begin.

The Greeks invented a monstrous theophany to express the invisible and we remain its victims far more than we think. That race of architects and sculptors suffered from an exaggerated tendency to see things in terms of mirror images. For them the temple was only a machine for looking at the world in order to cure it of contingency. The Jews, in contrast, knew that the invisible has never been seen. To see God is to die. The God made visible is an idolatrous image. That is why Jesus had to die, and after the resurrection had to go away in order that the Spirit might come and interiorize all things.

Similarly, the Palestinian world, unlike that of the Greeks, through a gigantic mime-drama, suggested the invisible in movement and life, poem and parable. Far from being overly fascinated by the real and instead of constructing magnified images of it, or exorcising it by means of metaphysical ideas, it fractures it, and remains on the lookout for passing moments and signs. During the exodus becomes blood, the storm-clouds are luminous. Water is changed into wine. In Jesus the Word is offered to be eaten and drunk. The invisible is in the heart of the real. It's impossible to believe, except in terms of magic, unless one goes through things and images. We believe with gestures, steps, the whole body.

The question isn't how to teach but how to live. Christianity doesn't exist in order to be known, and can be nothing but an intake of breath that will be quietly expelled, unless it temporarily creates slaves—those who simply recite the faith of others. The Gospel can only be the expression of an oral tradition in the movement and song of life. We don't teach anything to anyone; we only hand on that which gives us life.

Jousse tried to explain how in Aramaic Palestine the Word,

*Nemrâ*, was made flesh in a Galilean peasant and became the food of the teaching and the teacher.

"The final flowering of the pedagogy of the rabbi-peasant Yeshoua of Nazareth," he wrote, "is at the Last Supper, in the mime-drama of bread and wine where the teacher not only offers his teaching but himself as food and drink. . . . Here we have the most awesome expression of the primordial human mechanism."

# CHURCH

Like the storm-clouds of the exodus, the Church's face is more luminous today than when it seemed to rule. It has found glory in its humiliation.

Many people have believed in God through the agency of the Church. It now appears that, because of the Church, they no longer can. Undoubtedly that's because they have not encountered its submerged reality. Some of them, who have abandoned the second-rate faith they were taught, have become bold. Perhaps they are living the faith more authentically, as if they needed above all to get rid of borrowed ideas and feelings.

But someone who has been truly wounded by the Gospel, and has personally verified that the Church preaches the Word and makes the death and resurrection of Jesus present through the paradox of agony and contempt, can never find a pretext to desert. The one who leaves the Church proves he has never entered. Or, rather, he drags the Church along with him.


History lies. It retains only appearances and glorifies what is strong even when it is oppressive. And it neglects what is weak. It is the order of power. When history sees the Church surrender territory, often more because of the pressure of circumstances than because of greater spiritual profundity, it speaks of decadence or decline.

But wasn't the situation more disturbing when the Church functioned by anathemas and censures, or when, for example, Ciano and Gasparri signed the Lateran treaty, posing for a photo I've never forgotten, or when a Pope sincerely believed that in order to protect the flock it was better to stay within traditional diplomacy than to condemn Hitler's death camps directly? How much more ridiculous the Church was when Franco was awarded the Chain of the Order of Christ!

Faith makes us see everything differently. When the Church's prestige diminishes, when freedom shatters various forms of hypocrisy, when priests who for centuries have been under pressures that forced a large number to choose between a dishonest vocation and social disgrace are able to make their own decisions a little more freely, when churches begin to recognize that they can no longer use their political weight to influence moral decisions, there are clear signs of a Christian renaissance which, obviously, has nothing to do with social structures. Where did we get the idea that faith existed in order to prop up the social order of this world?

Why keep repeating "the Church of Christ, the Church of Christ"? Why are you so fearful? That Church, doesn't yet exist, and that's a matter for joy—we're still en route to Jerusalem. Let the Church become the Church of Christ; people will notice. But let it leave publicity to the popular advertisers who spend millions to influence opinion. To think that the Church could simply be illumination and light is absurd—fortunately! Otherwise, we'd already be in eternal life; admit you're not really keen on the idea.

Be suspicious of those who glory in belonging to the Church. It's not a matter of belonging. We are the Church on the march in all its diversity.

"Holiness," they say—"if only there were more holiness, everything would be simple!" They talk about sanctity the way others talk about oil. That's their style, naive and cunning. As if it were understood that holiness would leave everything the way it is.

How well-ordered and glorious the Church was in the days when Popes and cardinals waged war and practiced various other vices! Morality might receive a few setbacks but at least doctrine was never breached. That proved God was somehow present in it. When I was a boy apologetics knew how to make use of anything. How stupid! The time soon came when people could perceive that this doctrinal fortress was the symptom of dead minds that were only interested in control. The marvel was that the Word managed to make its way underneath all this, like a spring that is both protected and impeded by a large rock.

Yet now that Popes and cardinals and bishops are all holy men and no longer warriors, it appears there's nothing but disorder. "Is virtue fatal?" as Cioran asks. It's simply that the imperial order was the product of flesh and blood, partly justified by the doctrinal system. The interiorized, naked faith of today better reveals the contingency and humility of things—that is, the truth of the Christian condition.

### "The Tread of Beggars Will Make the Earth Tremble"

In his inaugural lecture at the Collège de France, Jean Delumeau called for a "history of hypocrisy in earlier centuries.... The Church," he said, "didn't 'lose' the working class; it never got that far."

The neat outline of a Christianity that reached a high point before declining further and further doesn't fit the facts. As soon as one replaces the pious approach to things with an historical one, this quickly becomes obvious. It was the kind of Christianity that arose during the Reformation and Counter-Reformation that caused the process of de-Christianization. The great masses of Christians experienced a religion mixed up with superstition and magic. Now their descendants, liberated from religious pressures and older customs and clinging to the rituals of success and the mythologies of the media, find such a mixture harder to accept. From the point of view of social morality this may represent a decline, but from a Christian perspective it's a gain, revealing the fact that only a small number were genuinely living the faith. To blame the Church for allowing itself to be expelled from its position is merely an attempt to maintain an illusion.

The Church has been overly concerned with itself, its order and its image, busying itself with what was not essential. What it helped to reveal to the world, directly or indirectly, has now entered into the common heritage of humanity. What does it matter if people want to forget where these values came from? What's important is to keep them alive and creative, even when they're hidden under the debris. It's hardly surprising that disciples all over the world seem no longer concerned with the Church but with poverty and human freedom. Every genuine community enlarges the Christian commonwealth.

If the Church, still moved by former reflexes, persists in trying to act directly on society instead of devoting itself completely to the spiritual development of its sons and daughters, its language will seem flabby and inadequate. Fortunately, it has neither the means nor the cynicism needed to get involved in the false battles of media ratings.

In the same way that Jesus' intention, clearly shown in the Gospels, was to lead each of us back to our center, it seems to me that the primary mission of Christianity is to rescue men and women who have been overcome by our present age and treated as mere consumers, and, whether they are politically active or not, to offer them a spiritual space. Everything else is insignificant.

The power of Bernanos' *Monsieur Ouine* remains in my memory. I can repeat pages by heart. Bernanos may still have dreamed of the older order of Christianity; the rest of us, minor Christian writers of the diaspora, no longer need that dream which was, after all, a mask for hope. But he touches us when he speaks of today's priest as one who "is all the more strange and hard to classify in that he will not admit that he is exceptional, nearly always himself the dupe of gross surface appearances, fooled by the ironic respect of some, the servile championship of others. But in the measure in which this contradiction, in any case more political than religious, from which their pride so long has drawn its sustenance, gets resolved by degrees into a kind of malicious indifference, the priest's ever-increasing sense of solitude impels him unarmed into the midst of social conflicts which the clergy fondly boasts it can solve with texts. But what does it matter? The hour is close upon us when, on the ruins of what is still left of our ancient Christian social order, the new order will be set up, that which will really be the rule of this world, the government of the Prince of this world, the Prince whose kingdom *is* of this world. And then under the harsh law of necessity this pride of churchmen, sustained so long by mere convention outlasting belief, will have lost even its own purpose—and beggars' feet will make the earth quake again."

## Am I a Liar?

How many times have I asked myself, "Am I a liar?" I was so far away from the pious atmosphere around me, its habits of mind, its vocabulary. But, to be honest, I am just as alien to the new language of the young Christian avant-garde who, in the illusion that consciences can be awakened only in the intellectual world, have locked themselves up again in the language of the scribes.

Shouldn't I simply have walked away on tiptoe and left for good? But where would I go? For me, outside the Church—what I called the Church, space for the Word—there was nothing: only closed systems which spoke about the organization of happiness, the future, work and leisure, more alienated even than religion. Nevertheless, I admit that for a while I was held back by the fear of failure. None of us are really very brave. But my experience also had taught me, contrary to the general opinion, that there was more freedom in the Church than anywhere else. I could see that for myself every day while watching how various factions and political parties operated. Of course, people thought of me as a special case—an artist, surrounded by books, flowers on the table, nothing to worry about. Above all, I had a few friends, some of them priests, a few politically active, dedicated to charitable projects, faithful but with few illusions, pure as diamonds, poor men and women who lived every day what I merely talked about. Through them I was part of the universal communion. Finally, last but not least, I knew that there were so many ordinary people—not just those old women who go to Mass every morning, but poor people, who might very well mix their faith with superstition and fear but who, whether through illusion or not, lived their lives entirely by means of the Church that exists here and now. What was one to offer them while waiting for the great day to come? I felt myself in solidarity with them as I followed my own route. I had lost the idealistic vision of a holy and spotless Church, which apologetics, playing with words, had set up in opposition to the real Church, but in seeing a handful of men and women—mediocre sinners like the rest of us, yet stubborn and active, dead set on the ultimate goal of love—I was compelled to place my confidence in it. What need did I have for certitude? The murmur of an interior word was enough, fragile, but constant in all seasons, a trickle from a source that speaks of innocence. I followed my inclination.

Today, because the Church is humiliated and dispersed, out of date in its techniques, and therefore encouraged to rediscover the naked word, I feel all the more indissolubly tied to it. But easy now, no pious proclamations; we never understand perfectly what influences us. Nevertheless, through my experience of the Church, I believe I've discovered a certain style of living and have worked through the problem by making the affirmation of Simone Weil my own: "I accept the Church's mission, as depositary of the sacraments and guardian of the sacred texts, to formulate decisions on some essential points, but only as directional signals for the faithful. I don't recognize its right to impose its interpretations."

Do we have to go over this again? I'd like to be able to say that we're not here to talk about my life, but Christianity. But how can we speak about it removed from experience without turning it into ideology? I'm quite aware that my experience is not necessarily a point of view that's closer to truthfulness. But precisely because of its fragility, it's less apt to impress people; it proceeds more by suggestion and encourages freedom.

## Trust the Troublemakers

I mustn't have had much imagination. For a long time I believed that the Church could only exist the way secular societies did. After all, wasn't the essential thing to be able physically to pass on the Word and the Eucharist? It didn't matter if the visible Church was a party to inhumanity. It was a question of incarnation. It was up to some of its children, who had been nourished by the Church, to live Christianity dangerously. But they'd better not expect the Church to run to their aid! It's more apt to reject them—except for beatifying them after death has made them inoffensive and useful. The harsh law of necessity prevailed in all this, as when superpowers disown their own spies. For what society would endure if it glorified the faithless steward, the prodigal son, the worker of the eleventh hour, and didn't wage war against its enemies? We'll believe almost anything in order to justify harmony and serenity!

During my visits to Rome I never set foot in the Vatican. By instinct, for fear of becoming a victim of irony and bitterness. However, a Roman bigwig who had read my work, and who frequently visited the troublemakers who were putting me up, offered to let me in on a few clerical coverups that he thought would spice up my novels. Unfortunately, I don't write romans à clef and have no desire to amuse the gallery. The miraculous lightness of Michelangelo's cupola was enough for me, along with Maderno's facade, and the columns on which Bernini, who had both humor and faith, had placed the saints.

How often I walked around the high walls, a thirty-minute hike, from which the Vatican seemed a gigantic shell, something absurd and necessary, at once a protection and a barrier. The fire shouldn't be allowed to flame too high. If the soul didn't have a body, there'd be no soul. If faith and love existed in perfect harmony, the world would dissolve into apocalypse. The image of Jesus dressed in a surplice, a crown on his head and a flower in his hand, never left me. People shouldn't get fascinated by light; they'll applaud the spectacular. The real action is interior. But there's always an obstacle, a scandal, to be overcome.

At a distance I observed a few ceremonies. The fire still smolders under the mask of formulas and rituals, I told myself, beyond the space for legalism. At the Easter vigil the paschal candle is used to light many others, and everyone leaves with a candle-stub. What does the imperial phantasmagoria matter, with its baroque splendor, century-old customs, all those cardinals, buddhas, bishops, protonotaries, and the army of priests who move by in procession—what does it all matter? It wasn't their job to change the order of the world, or even the order of the ceremony. Protected behind its walls, masked by its rituals, the Church—at least that Church—of prestige and authority was quite content to play worldly games, to maintain at great cost a diplomatic school that operated by standard police methods—including, I was told, hidden microphones—and to go on showing off its outdated Swiss guards, stimulating the faith of the people with ribbons, collars, and hats, hiding God behind dense liturgies, protocols, and sermons, just as he was hidden in the deepest hollow of destitution. But whoever had faith was able to hear the most lukewarm words and the darkest signs sparkled with light. We shouldn't take the whole set-up so seriously; faith and humor go well together.

The priests and bishops I knew were often completely without any mystical virus, endowed with solid good sense. I was prejudiced in favor of physical types who were immune to illusion, and led, I believed a secret interior life. I wanted to be like them. The stoic who I still was at that time was ready to justify almost anything, just as in another age I would have tolerated the holy Inquisition. The Gospel in its pure state was too great a danger. The old man in me still believes in that a little bit, especially since he's beginning to show his age. But that's no reason to listen to him. Remember: I'm writing this book at dawn, the hour of youth. The Church, I now believe, is invited to live a paradox—to break with the order of the world, to stop wanting to be a society complete in itself within civil society—in other words, a competitor, yielding or resisting depending on circumstances. It's impossible for the Church to make its message real unless its mode of presence is itself a sign.

Better to follow one's basic instincts. A Pope enshrined in his cope, crushed underneath his tiara, Jesus as President—all that looks odd on the screen; we don't know whether to laugh, feel pity, or get angry. Trust your gut reactions. I can recognize the humiliated Jesus, a reed in his hand. But a Pope who would abandon the Holy See, who would get rid of the finery and all that it signifies, live in a tenement slum and direct some kind of international labor union, would worry me even more. I don't know what style the Church should have. I only want what is written to begin to come to completion. Style is a bonus.

## Unity in Nudity

We go on trips, taking notes while passing through half-starving continents where cadavers are piled up each morning along with the garbage. We no longer can put up with the parable of the good Samaritan. Faith becomes impossible, nothing is what it used to be, but we go on cultivating the moral garden of the West!

It's obvious that the Church is not catholic but Western.

"Unity in nudity," Jabès says.

In the old days one was born with a ready-made morality that did our thinking and deciding for us. It was an immense help, but it was

155

also a drug and an iron collar. The morality that was considered Christian, and which was largely accepted even by those who were not believers, became natural. Those days are over, splintered in a thousand directions. It's a stroke of luck: faith can now rid itself of foreign elements, rediscover its daring, and become once again the seed of life.

The magisterium has often condemned doctrines that naturalized faith but has usually tried to avoid genuine confrontation. What indignation when believers—who don't always believe for genuine reasons—are persecuted! It's laughable. Because of compromise Christianity doesn't appear in its truth—a truth that is often unacceptable. It is revealed only in tension and debate, provided that it's not looking for power and prestige. In the bosom of the reigning order, whichever it is, Christianity can only be in search of another order, both peaceful and rebellious.

The Church is something quite different than the guardian of a doctrine and a morality in the social sense of the word. It's that portion of humanity, visible or invisible, in which God, to the degree that images of his mythic representation were effaced, has found more space to advance than elsewhere—the God of the burning bush, of Abraham. It's the communion of all those, neither the best nor the worst, whose gaze is focused on the far distance, who seem to be pointing to a human territory where the night is a little less dark and who help us believe that dawn will break in that direction.

The true universality of the Church consists in its ability to root itself in particular situations and to rise above them, arousing the effective love which shows itself without distinction among a certain number of men and women whose inner voice is in harmony with the Word and who appear as witnesses.

The movement toward unity is irreversible. Formerly I used to ask myself if I were part of the true Church. The question went back, like so many false questions, to childhood. The true, universal Church is not the one that affirms its will to be so, but the one that, without being too interested in itself, communicates the faith in love to everyone. So it's not primarily here or there. The Church exists everywhere there are communities that give testimony of universal love. Unless language changes—and it changes only after a spiritual revolution—ecumenism will remain what it has seemed so far, an administrative enterprise, following the laws of competition in which, despite the vocabulary of good feeling, we always detect the prudent search for advantage. We don't want to be cynical, but the truth is that no one wants to lose his clientele. Ecumenism will become truly worldwide only by rejecting calculation, through self-effacement.

In general, we think of traditions as we do of things: institutions, formulas, habits. In these terms the Church would be an aggregate of objects—in which traditions created men. That's how materialism can wear the mask of fidelity. An exaggerated reverence is often attached to a very recent past, while progressivism hurls itself into the future. Every genuine spiritual renewal, however, arouses a spirit directed at that instant in which past and future are connected. That's where tradition really is.

How can we pass on the faith? That's the way we used to pose the question. We're here, possessors of the truth, and the others are there. In such a context, whether the testimony is dramatic or discrete, it leads to a dead end.

It's impossible, in however roundabout a way, to impose a morality of repression by baptizing it as Christian. We must reject all the conjuring tricks that would burden consciences with fear, culpability, and self-importance and call the whole thing faith. The only way to proceed is to recognize each human being in his or her truth, in terms of lived moralities, over and above everything else that may be similar or different. All that is said is never anything but a preliminary gesture in order that faith might be created, almost without our trying.

The logic of faith is to disentangle itself from every kind of hypocrisy and pious ideology—that is, from death. When Christianity is simply what it is and nothing more it will be on an even footing with all humanity, with the scattered crowd of all those who seek something better, whether blindly or clearsightedly.

It will pay for this, of course.

The Christian doesn't wear any particular label. Since she's like everyone else, she can be recognized only insofar as she believes that a door opens on to the absolute and tries to live out the implications of this. Nothing rigid. Giving military commands was the style in the old days when believers represented so many battalions and Christendom lived by the fiction of large numbers. But Christian faith is creative because it is a faith, not an imitation or a phantom of faith. Whether an individual is convinced by one ideology or another doesn't matter. By a spiritual instinct she knows that we are not made for the sabbath. Spontaneously at the service of people, because she likes to be, she is the presence of the Church, without necessarily knowing it or wanting it.

I see the Church discovering a style. Let it cease to tire itself out by repeating laws and principles. Let the Church give life to its own, to those who come to it freely and joyously. Let them grow in the good and evil of life in this world of horse-racing, lotteries, TV, and pornography. There's no time to lose by fighting all that. Vice is natural, futility is natural. Let the Church provide the powerful nourishment of the Word, which is always critical, but at a deeper level. I see the Church detaching its members from structures of profit, conventional security, and mythologies of happiness in order to make them spiritual nomads, capable of commitment without illusion, always ready to absent themselves in order to go somewhere else, straining for the impossible and necessary.

Such joyous men and women exist, capable of invention and fantasy, both close by and far away, unpredictable, alone or in hundreds of scattered communities. The thousand hearts of the world *koinonia* beat in them.

## Get Rid of Statistics

Here is this partly nomadic Church, a scattered presence. Is it here, there? God will recognize his own. It has no cause to defend, no flag. Demobilization has taken place. Such a Church is nearer to us, unpredictable. Fewer people believe that they are proprietors of certain concepts. Communities come to birth all over its great body, grow, then disband in order to reform elsewhere, differently; there are miracles, cures, scandals—everything takes place in the open, testimonies of a burning love. There's an acceptance of the provisional in a world that suffers from a security syndrome, anticipating the security of cemeteries. The Church is in movement, unified but seemingly in a thousand fragments, strong in its fragility, around the central kernel, with a solid head. Would I talk this way if I hadn't seen so many men and women who no longer worried about how to accommodate the message or what techniques to use but lived the Gospel in their own lives? I no longer think in the official language. I recognize a voice that emerges from the centuries. It has a source somewhere, which we can't see—in the growing grass, the tree-frog's croak, the bird's wing.

Yes, the Church needs a solid head, but cured of the dignity of officialdom and acts of folly. There is general absolution: everyone comes to the banquet. The nuptial robe is the final end of all those who advance in the darkness with the help of nothing but a candlestub. An interior wisdom. Heresy is eliminated of itself, like the dead trees of the forest. Let life break its chains, create; all this energy will be channeled soon enough. It's better than having lots of canals without living water. There's no great need to know what will happen afterward.

We've lived too long with the idea of large numbers. Life makes up only a small part in the huge mass of matter, thought is fragile within the groaning of life, and love is so fragile in the midst of the conceited creations of the mind. Pascal has said it for always: matter only has meaning in life, life in thought, and thought in love.

Whatever shows itself in the light of day begins as a passion in the consciousness of an individual. None of us realize our own resources. The more we reach into the basket, the more bread there is. We give what we don't have.

David, after having fixed the frontiers of his people, wanting to make an inventory of his goods and calculate his power, took up statistics. He is condemned in the First Book of Chronicles, in the Second Book of Samuel. Of course, the Bible knows how to count— seven, forty, a thousand, ten thousand—but it counts in symbolic numbers, because it's telling a story that goes beyond mere story.

Understand this paradox. On one hand, salvation is universal and hence is aimed at all humanity; on the other hand, its message calls for intimate commitment. That's the way things are in the spiritual order. Leaven has to be leaven: that's the only thing that will lift up the mass. Pressure techniques are the worst kind of betrayal. "Go, teach ye all nations"—but you have to preach inner change.

The temptation is insidious. It's risky and time-consuming to place one's confidence in spiritual power. To avoid solitude and misunderstanding it's more convenient to use the powerful means that are available today for communicating faith as an opinion. An apostle who begins to build a structure is lost, or saved. Dread may keep him awake; interior life could be liquidated. The leaven is imprisoned under the shell of his good works.

After Vatican II the Church tried to improve its image. Instead of posing the question "How are we to live?" which calls for a transformation in the way we see, they asked, "What should we say?" A Christianity that was supposed to be avant-garde, activist, anti-mystical, wanted to regain revolutionary energies in order to do the same kind of thing as the official Church, but from a different starting-point.

Indoctrination, publicity, and recruiting—in which established

Christendom excelled—has spread monstrously, as much in the West as in the East. The battle of the media has been lost—but that's a gain. Apostles are forced to settle down somewhere else when they realize the worship of large numbers is a lie.

To want to bring the Gospel back to its source—to let it be difficult, to refuse to turn it into cultural gruel—is this showing scorn for simple people? For how many years I've heard that refrain. The simple people, it's worth saying once more, have a spontaneous affinity for spiritual things. It is the enlightened ones, rather, who think they possess the meaning of the message and keep cooking up gruel for the unsophisticated. They're the ones who show contempt by treating people like dunces and justifying the repression and guilt which consolidate their power. When I hear them I think of an old man leaning over a child and using baby talk; there's an ironic gleam in the eyes of the child that says, "Lay off, dummy!"

Genuine love of men and women is shown first by rejecting the crowd as such. That's what the Gospel does: it leaves the love of humanity to politicians.

## How Do We Live in the Meantime?

That's the key question. Passionate love is only a momentary eruption if it's not expressed in fidelity. But fidelity can just as easily mean ossification as love. Concepts, doctrines, and ideology are means that are also obstacles, providing an anchor of security against the drift. The Word attacks this kind of security. Concepts, doctrines, and ideology have no reason to worry; they're secreted by desire and fear, which are eternal. There can never be an end to the spiritual combat between those who provide anchors and build foundations for us and others who wish to lead us into the desert.

The same holds true for any institution. The effervesence of our age undermines it but is simultaneously spurred in search of it. Resentment alone causes the institution temporarily to reject this ferment. For Christian existence, like existence in general, can't remain suspended in a vacuum. Otherwise, how would it avoid dissolution and a sense of unimportance? Only spiritual logic requires institutions to really open themselves to the universal in spite of concrete differences. Their basic character should encourage such an awakening, since faith is always a beginning, a succession of beginnings.

To write against myself: Christianity is not necessarily mystical.

Moreover there is a deluxe mysticism, a perception of awareness and inner peace that one finds in the Tao and in Hinduism as well as in the Gospel. This can be merely a cultural phenomenon to justify and extend life.

Believers who are mystics have always been a lowly race, repressed for a long time. Such confidence, and obedience not necessarily passive, is the path of a very different race of people who are in touch with the absolute. They are usually people of silence, without necessarily being quiet. They show a certain healthiness, a disinterest in religion and doctrinal abstractions that will save them. They start off in the right direction. It seems to be enough for them to believe without too many illusions in the spiritual experience of their Church. Although they've never had an interior illumination, a loving faith is at the center of their life.

All this is true, but it is also becoming evident that in a society that is out of joint and has no direct spiritual experience, the credibility of the Christian disappears. When the structures are relaxed and the flock is dispersed, when light no longer comes from on high, collective faith has to become individual; each of us has to make his or her own reading of the event as it appears to us.

Every time I've heard the Credo sung by a crowd, it seemed to be against something or other. As a child, it was against the secularism of the state schools. I remember listening to a talk by a certain general: the Credo that followed moved me to tears of faith.

But those who use the Credo today to defend the old Church deceive themselves only because they have been deceived. The hierarchy should have avoided upsetting them. After all, it was the Church which, instead of educating them, mobilized them. Let them have their Latin! The bishops should have shown more caution before getting rid of treasures. Just as the institutional Church was intolerant of the avant-garde until the moment when, through a conjuring trick, they became the majority, so intolerance has rebounded on the reactionaries. Instead of letting their consciences ripen, the Church took the way of authority. It's another clear sign of spiritual infantilism.

That's no reason for not looking at certain realities without pity. Pity is appropriate for dealing with individuals, not situations. Just as there used to be an inability to read the Bible except with an official interpretation, there's a comparable inability to understand certain aspects of reality.

For a long time now, for example, marriages and baptisms in many sectors of the population are only the residue of social conservatism.

They not only do not "transmit" faith but are an obstacle to it. Nevertheless, sacramentalism persists in the minds of many people: to get baptized or married in church is reassuring. The refusal to risk a policy of baptizing at an age when it would be an adult act is concealed by pious notions that also hide the desire for conquest. We ought to recognize that many men and women of our time, when they eliminate every trace of their baptism, experience a sense of liberation.

It is also becoming evident that for many people, to follow a civil marriage with a religious marriage no longer seems a sign of spiritual commitment. Voices are raised, reforms suggested; every year new initiatives are taken, which sometimes give scandal. These are false scandals which keep specialists and onlookers busy for a while, preventing them from thinking about what is at the heart of it all: the lack of spiritual realism, the fear of accepting a Christianity that would be fervent and free. Because that would make it necessary to base everything on genuine faith and apparently lose many of the large crowd who still hang on.

It's hardly surprising that so many families are frantic to keep up "traditions" of indoctrination and ritual. Not living the faith profoundly within themselves, their Christianity contains neither vigor nor joy; it's therefore not very contagious, since their notion of communion is only nostalgic. When it's a matter of interior necessity, they talk about letting everything go and surrendering, so as to avoid thinking about the desert of their own existence.

### Successors of the Apostles

We need to relearn the sense of the temporary. Of a people joyously en route. "Leave your country, and your kindred, for the land that I will show you." New songs, constantly recreated as the songs of life. Everything begins this very instant.

The prophet versus the wordly leader. We need a form of *authority*—author, one who gives life (the author of my days), who increases it—a chief if you prefer, but without power.

If the Church were an army, the hierarchical system as it now functions would be extremely efficient. For the strength of an army is generally related to the commitment and ambition of its officers and junior officers; they're totally available.

But the Church is nothing like an army. If its leaders are merely a driving belt, powered, whether they know it or not, by fear, making them look first to see how the wind blows, or are driven by some vanity that may have the appearance of obedience and devotion, they are only caricatures of the apostles. No communion is built on directives and compromises but on an inner experience of liberation.

Sons of peasants, fishermen, businessmen, and lawyers, I know you and your love of Jesus, your passion for goodness and your anguish. I know your disinterestedness, your ability, your prudence, and even your ambition. You have placed them at the service of Mother Church and believe yourselves justified. Not everyone has that opportunity.

I'm just back from a mission to the outsider, Your Excellencies, from a world without pity. I've crawled around in the underground, often without bread or water. Of course, you can disown me; I made a deal with the enemy, acted as a double agent. One of you gave me this mission a long time ago in a cathedral while litanies were being recited. Listen: as Bernanos says, "It's not my song that is eternal, but what I sing"—and that does not belong to me.

Nevertheless, when I take this haughty tone in addressing bishops no one should think that I have lessons to teach anyone. I observe, and invent a new way of accepting the world so as not to lose heart. I realize that one can never tell anyone else to do this or that, or reproach someone for anything, without being a hypocrite. Everything arrives in its own time, from within. I point out symptoms. I let my natural buoyancy run free.

I suspect they think being present in the world means getting involved in all those ideological debates and shouting from the rooftops. Of course avoiding the futility of debate doesn't justify being absent when it's a question of justice and freedom. But let their voices come from far away, from an unknown world, surprising us; let them become a source of inspiration for their own people instead of blabbing about everything, impeccably.

Stop talking about the decline of faith; no more blackmail about orthodoxy or calls to close ranks. Be disinterested in everything that's not essential. One has to go through the passage from illusion to reality. To chew on nothingness. To be a refugee from vanities. To see through the tricks of vocabulary. A critical thought without pious fat, not shriveled up with fine phrases but open to the fullness of the Word—it would be a recovery of the spirit of childhood. That spirit only begins beyond the tragic and joyous perception of life and is the opposite of childishness.

Some of my friends became successors of the apostles. I soon took my distance from them, not out of a conscious decision but because of the absence of a common language.

Men who become bishops are generally intelligent and sensitive. Troublemakers, of course, aren't predisposed to that vocation but bishops are neither better nor worse than others. Before their "elevation" they are often quite critical of the hierarchy. But as soon as they are promoted their statements become trivial. After a few outbursts, their language grows diplomatic; aiming at everyone, it touches no one.

Brought together like business leaders in order to issue forecasts, they seem to cancel each other out. Their texts are the calculated result of compromise, reasonable products which may well contain truth but have no roots in flesh.

I'm going to say something that's painful, to me first of all. A bishop had just been named—he had wanted the appointment very much. It's not true that ambition dies; no one gets to be bishop without having wanted it, or almost no one. As soon as he was appointed, he stopped being fraternal, although fraternity still showed in his face and his hands. He was filled with good will, but at the same time his shoulders sagged under the weight of the world and he was submerged in apostolic agony. His vocabulary grew stereotyped, deliberate. His speeches fell into easy clichés.

Don't jump to the conclusion that I'm bitter. Neither you nor I am important in this matter; it's simply my voice you're hearing. Every morning at dawn, as I write, I listen to Bach; don't you notice its serenity? I'm speaking to you from the depth of my soul, without any shame. Firm and friendly, an accomplice.

For thirty years I have heard these things said by mature diocesan priests, men who have sharp eyes, sometimes sharp teeth, who were far from being yes-men. They didn't have theories but experience. They knew that as soon as a bishop had power he began to come apart, and they also realized that it was almost none of his own doing. They laughed about it; I did, too. There's a time for everything. Today is a different time. Hope is violent, as you well know.

I'm not saying that other celebrities, who perform in different rings of the world circus, are more appealing. On the contrary, I'm prejudiced in favor of the apostles because they're married to the Word and to eternity. But for that very reason we expect a certain style from them. I call style a way of occupying space, of directing one's glance and one's voice, of existing, that's produced by an interior discovery.

Pardon me—one day I took you by surprise as I passed through the hubbub you made in leaving some important meeting and overheard

164

shreds of your conversation. You were among your own; we all need a break. For an instant I thought it was a shame that you had given up red and violet for a fine suit, and that the old uniform had its virtues.

Get together again, Your Excellencies, and deal with the essential questions. You have eliminated many things, veiled the signs of wealth, shortened your trains, bought less conspicuous cars, sold off the furniture and sometimes even the episcopal palace—how expensive all that vanity was! But what is still to be done is more serious. "The truly poor man is the one who knows nothing," Meister Eckhart says.

Don't pass on a message composed of truths that have been discussed in committee, but an experience that would be intimate enough to spark communion. Don't try to verify prior assumptions by facts but look at the facts.

You worry me because you never make mistakes. Make mistakes; you'll have more opportunities to be just and true.

Above all, don't hold on to power for long, since your authority is also power. Exercise it, leave, and return to the ranks—that's a beginning.

When you see a religious celebrity, a sought-after speaker, a master of the spiritual life, using all his energy to pursue some honor, don't say anything, just laugh. Monkeys climb trees. People are always going to be moved by a flood of words, knowledge, and piety. Everything leads back to nothing. And don't admire individuals! They may be humble and poor for themselves and still be innocently pursuing the game of prestige and power. Such innocence is worse than anything else. When deception runs so deep it's impossible to uncover. But one thing is obvious: worldly honors, whether religious or not, grow like poisonous mushrooms after the rain.

Those who proclaim a full word today are more apt to emerge from the night. *I will lose the wisdom of the wise.* And even if, unexpectedly, an official who hasn't yet traded in his soul tears a living word from his very being, it won't be heard—the past is too heavy. The space doesn't yet exist in which it would resound in the ears of outsiders. Above all, Your Excellencies, be suspicious of those who turn back to you to say that they're good children who believe in everything; they only intensify the darkness.

Mouthpieces of the dead, parrots, tenants of thoughts that were already thought, instead of having been nourished and supported by pain and joy, less successors than walk-ons for the apostles—that's how the leaders of the Church appear in the eyes of outsiders. And yet the outsider I speak of is prejudiced in favor of them. The interior murmur that speaks of the absolute hasn't left him. But it's impossible to make him hear unless you yourselves become outsiders.

What a powerful message could be announced today! On condition that the apostles abandon both the false struggles and those combats which are not their own. Theirs is the spiritual combat "more harsh than the battles of men." Let them stop agonizing about economic and social questions, the family and the birthrate. Let them allow their "faithful" in their diversity to blend in with life. Transformation of mind and heart, interior justice, that's what concerns apostles. In this world that is prey to the exaggeration of desires and hopes as well as to the scientific pseudo-rationality of progress that culminates in the absurd, they must give a sign that salvation is also and above all in the hearts of each of us, in all the ordinary places of life—the interior space of disinterestedness and serenity.

As long as the priest is primarily a functionary of the sacred, the professional of the parade-ground—that is, as long as he constitutes a caste—Christian communities will not arrive at real responsibility any more than the soldiers of a regiment, in spite of all the adjustments made under the pressure of circumstances.

Whether the priesthood should entail obligatory celibacy, whether women should be ordained, from now on priesthood will more and more imply a vocation born from within, a passion. It's a bishop who issues the call; one does not give it to oneself. In itself this realism has always seemed to me to show great wisdom, but for a long time it has been allowed to mask inattention and a kind of abandon. Certain economic and psychological mechanisms have produced an assembly-line priesthood.

Quite a few priests have told me my books have helped them. Some have persevered because of them, they said, others have left, still others have been unable to make a real choice because of various factors. In this way I found out about the sum of illusions that were fostered and the dishonesty and pain caused by an idealistic representation of things.

Freely chosen priestly celibacy was a fantastic power for giving and loving. It helped form a large number of fraternal men who helped slaves, women, and the poor to exist—those who felt the need to breathe more freely. Making celibacy a requirement for the priesthood has poisoned and falsified innumerable consciences and led to the over-compensation of activism when it didn't produce a fanatical faith that was merely the crystallization of despair. It has been a deadly policy for some time. Before thinking of "the good of the Church" in the short term, or at least what is considered as such in conceptualist and administrative terms, it would be better to think of the freedom of men. In this area many things have been preserved only by the torture of some and the hypocrisy of others. It was undoubtedly one of the causes of the weakness and sadness of the Christian world just before so many priests "deserted."

There is no crisis of vocations.

There are more genuine vocations, in small numbers. The call never stops. Young people want to respond—I've met them. All of them weren't rich. They weren't leaving because they were rich. Sometimes the clerical atmosphere bothered them. Some embraced Marxism and then left it for the same reasons that they had halted on the threshold of the Church.

The apostle of our time does not have the social prestige of earlier times; he is incapable of glorying in his role or crying victory, thereby arousing envy or hostility. Living more deeply, he experiences his own unbelief so well that he is the brother of atheists and unbelievers, not just in intention and words—that is, in illusion. The Word of the Gospel and of the Church has become so much his own that he is like a humble innkeeper who rejects no one, whom one feels the need to visit, whether to be quiet or to talk, just as one visits a healer or a guru—although he has nothing in common with a guru. Lucid, cured of many hopes and fears, no more virtuous than anyone else, capable of solitude and silence, without need of recognition, skilled in reading on someone's lips words other than those that were spoken, in gently uncovering the lie within sincerity, he's not afraid of enjoying himself, without which one can't give to anyone else.

*The way of the master* is inscribed in the Gospel and in the very nature of the "inner" Christianity revealed "to the apostles and the little ones"; this makes it possible for them to avoid the illusion of general ideas proper to that external Christianity that only reaches the mind, when it reaches anything. The master reveals God and eternal life in sympathy, in the very instant, not through an abstract morality that leaves us foreign and indifferent when it doesn't produce guilt.          ·

## Do You Want To Be Baptized in the Spirit?

The old organism is on the move and is growing young again, some would say.

People had thought that the secret tradition revealed to the apostles and the poor in anticipation of the final revelation, which blossomed in the first centuries within an orthodox gnosticism, had become definitively reserved to monasteries and a few privileged individuals. On the one hand, the traditional Church might well be the Church of saints, but it seems like the Church of dead saints, a prisoner of a systematically functional thought, unable to speak the language of the living. Despite the appearances of renewal, one might have said that evangelical charisms had been completely absorbed by ritual. On the other hand, a minority of activist Christians, anti-mystical, no doubt because after so many centuries of confusion they couldn't avoid mistaking mysticism for idealism, seemed to be motivated only by social causes and to want, above all, to adapt the Gospel to our time. But it's not enough to transform apostles into community organizers, to have Jesus enter Jerusalem on a motorcycle, or to turn Simon of Cyrene into an immigrant worker. It's right to admire the generosity and rigor of activists and agree with their criticisms of Christian society. But at the same time something is missing: they believe too much in their own analyses and proposals, they identify too much with human hopes. It all lacks fantasy, humor, and ultimately, interior freedom—eternal life here and now.

But now a new fervor has arisen. A new springtime, in a large number of communities of prayer. At last something surprising is happening, which is unsettling. The conceptual and rational are, in general, not rejected, but there's something that overflows such limits. We're dealing with emotion instead of a dissertation on social planning; spiritual boldness has replaced hesitation. Here is a commitment that involves more than concepts and phrases, and suggests a kind of connaturality.

Some men and women seem to be experiencing joy. In their lives there is a before and an after. Before the Spirit arrived there had been excessive concentration on some sorrow or desire, a frenetic pursuit of success, and everything was tangled up and lifeless. After, a simplification had taken place, producing a buoyant confidence. Such people go through difficulties without, so to speak, noticing them. Human relationships again become possible, along with attention to others, genuine encounters. It's as if prayer were producing visible fruits. In itself this experience is as much opposed to the ossification of reactionaries as to the constant activism of the progressives.

Nevertheless, I admit wanting to get away during some of their prayer meetings, and sometimes I did so. Too much honey and at-

168

mosphere; too much "Jesus is Lord." All those tape-recorders that were always on, not to mention the young girls who rolled on the ground with laughter. And too many tears.

Our souls have been weighed down for so long with reserve, tamed by smooth, tranquil services, that when the body begins to express itself freely we go back into our shells. We just want peace to reign, right? Or do we, to insure our inner comfort, come down on the side of censure and repression? None of this confusion, more clarity! One never knows what such simplicity may be hiding.

Several days were needed before I could question my first reflexes. But I have met too many wounded idealists and knew my power-lessness to help them—or, rather, help them to help themselves—not to rejoice that some people were able to find a place to express themselves. It was less expensive than psychoanalysis. Is it better for unhappy people to keep wearing their masks? For whom is it better? Isn't anything better than lies and hypocrisy based on fear? Or must emotionalism be sidetracked into drugs and suicide? Besides, in this overly-programmed world in which we live, it seemed marvelous to me that there were zones of foolishness—and perhaps liberation and grace—where human beings, forgetting about economic growth and consumer comforts, could speak freely of their desire for beatitude.

To explain all this in terms of auto-suggestion and group dynamics seemed too simple to me. Why not first accept human reality in its diversity and with all its ambiguities: miracles or pseudo-miracles, speaking in tongues or the gift of tongues? It's not my job to make judgments, even if I retain a strong dose of skepticism and humor in regard to the external signs of spiritual richness.

Certainly the innumerable invocations, the constant affirmation that one is living with the Lord (as if it were necessary to convince oneself), the exalted joy or calm—such things can be a perfectly iden-tifiable product of over-compensation, a flash in the pan, the new sense of belonging to a group, and escape from responsibility. The benevolent attitude of some members of the hierarchy to the char-ismatic movement gives grounds for concern. "Those fine souls," some may be thinking, "they're obedient, and they pray; they won't cause us any embarrassment with political involvement. It's un-likely they'll shake up any institutions. Let's follow them; after all, we're their leaders."

The danger is that these new communities might serve as an alibi and put up with traditional dualism by distinguishing between the things of God and the things of the world, in the vague idea that everything will be solved by the Holy Spirit. But it's clear that if faith can't simply be identified with human hope, neither can it be built up against it by substituting charity for the necessary struggle for human liberation.

All the same, the thought came to me that it's neither good sense nor stoicism which makes for discernment, but the second intelligence, a sort of infallible, instinctive intelligence that the Holy Spirit gives and "that we all have received," as it says in the Acts of the Apostles. The Holy Spirit is not necessarily linked to miracles or prophecy, as Paul reminds us in 1 Corinthians, but to active love and our general life-orientation.

It's not a matter, therefore, of bringing a movement into line but of nourishing it, harmonizing spiritual vitality and a critical attitude within a living tension. On this condition the charismatic movement should be able to bring life to the old Church, to rid it of its shoddy intellectualism and the ideologies that have become confused with the faith, and at the same time help bring this branch of new apostles to fruition.

But finally, as always, it was the unexpected encounters rather than remarks overheard that made it impossible to turn away and helped me to be fair.

There was a doctor, still young but already well-established, avid to grasp a fistful of cash each evening to prove he was alive. He bore all the external signs of success and wealth. It had been his misfortune or happiness to attend a prayer meeting. And see what happened: he decided a few months later, together with his wife, to leave the city and join a dispersed community in a remote village. There, he would not even tell people he was a doctor but simply do useful work, exercising his profession only if a doctor were needed in the area. What a bad example! What would happen if everyone did the same? But there's nothing to worry about; you know that very well. Something like prayer had taken hold of him. You never know.

Gabrielle, about thirty-five, has a twelve year old daughter. Her husband is a successful businessman. She attended prayer meetings without much enthusiasm; out of loyalty, he had gone with her. One day she asked for the laying on of hands.

"Why do you wish to receive the baptism of the Spirit?"

"To break away from egoism, to be delivered from the demon of acquisition."

There were no lightning flashes. Days went by, and then she asked herself "What's the point of all this money?" and there was a stab of pain deep in her breast. The rest of us turn on TV, see the refugees on the road, the swollen bellies of African children, and we feel emotions, we have ideas and opinions. Not she; she proceeds to action. In succession she and her husband adopt a little Algerian girl, a little Vietnamese girl, and a two year old French boy who had become deaf and dumb because of beatings he had undergone. I listen, I watch. There is no trace of tension or exaltation. She performs her miracles naturally. Her husband, her daughter, and everyone else follow, then go on ahead.

I hardly dare talk about Gerda. Her story risks throwing suspicion on the others. Her life is spent among fashion models. She's in charge of the fashion section of a very successful journal. Statuesque, radiant, sophisticated. Why had she gone to a few prayer meetings? She had been dragged along by a friend. Had she experienced a thunderclap? No, more a feeling of strangeness, followed by a delayed reaction. A thought persists for months at work, something like the universal vanity of all things, until the day when, to everyone's amazement, she quits. She went to see a priest to ask which was the strictest order of women. She entered the Poor Clares. A few days before she left, she organized a benefit for the third world. Everything went: robes, furs, fancy furniture.

Was this an escape from life? A disappointment in love? It didn't look that way. For some years she had been very close to a Tunisian; they separated by mutual agreement without a big scene. The amazing thing is that all her Christian friends, except one, were very much against her decision to enter the convent. They talk about the love of God, the absolute, and eternal life, but if someone starts acting on all that, they resist. Is it so terrible to enter eternity while still alive? They say what people usually say in such a case: she won't last. They reassure themselves as much as they can. I waste my time on the other side of the grille looking for something in her voice or her eyes, to see if I can spot some protective illusion. All I can make out is a solid peace. Are we realists so sure of not being enclosed in our neurosis of happiness? It's true that her face, framed by her long hair, was made to be painted. Bare, it seems to cry out with poverty. I cannot say that Gerda doesn't frighten me, but I love the insolence of the Holy Spirit, if it's the Spirit.

A rigorously Thomistic theologian collapsed during a prayer meeting at which he was merely an observer. He actually shed tears. Of course, in itself that doesn't prove a thing. He was a serious man with a distinguished reputation, someone who knew what was just, orthodox, or dangerous. Now he laughs at his former wisdom. I've heard him say, "Throw ideas in the garbage!" He goes too far; besides, he has a sense of humor. But I think I can guess what he means without having it explained: that philosophy as such only leads up to creation and merely demonstrates its own logical perfection. To adhere truly to the uncreated God, one must be nourished by him, obscurely present in creation, certainly, but incarnated in Jesus Christ who lives in us through the Spirit. And it is in this "knowing" that we know the world and ourselves. Without it, in mere conceptual phenomena, we are able to perceive only absurdity or nothingness.

# INSTANT

Why do I get involved with all this—concepts, ideology, institutions? Never again. But how could I do otherwise? If you start off in a poetic vein, you find yourself alone. People look at you as if you're odd. Hardly anyone wants "truths made for the feet, truths that can dance." You tell yourself that you'll play their game only in order to educate them, and find yourself caught in the trap. The book stirs up too much conceptual sediment. My desk and bookshelves have been empty for years, but how do you stop trying to be clever and simply tell those closest to you what keeps you going? My hope is that some young people might be both wounded and cured by the tiny touch between the lines and which can never be put into words.

I was in the middle of writing this when a letter arrived from Sarah, an Englishwoman I didn't know. She has a Russian name and has lived in France for a long time. She says that a new faith is rising in Soviet Russia, which they call "Break-Rock," because it sprouts up in the fissures of rock. It has little in common with Aleksandr Solzhenitsyn who, despite his great courage, represents "an old faith filled with nostalgia and resentment." That's why the West extols him, she says, because "the West extols only dead thoughts." Break-Rock is a serene faith that has grown up in the cracks of the Soviet confessional state which has taken the place of the Czarist state-god. This faith is not shocked at being confronted with what is anachronistic and finds it natural that Christianity should be secret and dangerous because, fortunately, it's not accustomed to having power.

Sarah says that she hears in my books a voice of secret hope, "as if you're writing about another time, a foreign country. To live each day with passion, joy, and freedom, as if it's the last, our eyes open to sadness, is that what it's like," she asks, "to walk into the sun of death? Or is it just the magic of language? I'd like to know."

Could the desire to live be strong enough, Sarah, to produce the poem, the beyond, and God, to give us joy in being part of the world, like a kid who dresses up as an Indian and pretends he's in Texas, so that our absolute is crepe-paper and represents sheer craziness, the need to have a halo, to be important in our own eyes? If that's the case, how absurd it would be to fight against the wall of ideas; they are our only salvation if everything rests on emptiness.

There's nothing to understand, Sarah. No proof is given except that "In the beginning was the Word," that it has come among us, that it lives in the humility of bread and the Word, that some of us place our confidence in it without proof, except that it overcomes idols and offers superabundant life.

And now, friends who have followed me, let me play my tunes once more, since they are also yours. Whether they're songs of illusion or reality is not our business. Music knows better than we do, leading us where we didn't want to go.

If, nevertheless, the movement that impels me is foreign to you, don't be worried. No person can understand thoughts that she doesn't already bear in herself. Perhaps a day will come when the world will sparkle before you, the visible and the invisible, the atrocious and the radiant, everything given and taken back, with you inside it tiny and joyous, present and absent, almost like God who directs the universe while remaining foreign to it. Don't be afraid to leave the spectacle behind, along with the guilt and the categorical imperative, and turn toward a joyous life. You'll communicate more happiness by living than you will with all your hard work and prudence. Only don't set out expecting to get first place at the feast or to be honored by second-raters with established reputations.

Are you capable of keeping your distance and looking closely at the societies you're living in? Like penned-up cattle, numbered and branded, you too have been given a number at the police station, by your teacher, at Social Security, and everywhere else, all for your own good, and soon cameras will observe you through your television set. You may have repressed Providence and God, but the all-powerful state sees all, knows all, and loves you enough to communicate to you, morning, noon, and night, at every instant, the slogans and prevailing ideas that constitute your quasi-obligatory spiritual nourishment, and the same state will select your books and images according to the laws of quantity and the short-term market, which are also the laws of money. This state-god loves you to the point of permitting a number of ideologies to be expressed at the same time; therefore, you are free. You have the beautiful freedom of being able to say only yes or no, as if these directly opposed positions are not like two peas in a pod.

Haven't you understood?

The West is the third world of the spirit. Its sadness can't be fathomed; it's the sadness of those who are separated from themselves, insatiable. The poverty and destitution of the third world still leaves room for fraternity in collective agony. In the West agony is individual. Old and young, sick and handicapped—all are placed in the charge of specialists but are irredeemably alone. If we were logical, we would park them in reserved zones. But this Western framework will surrender only to spiritual assault. Technocratic rearrangements are insignificant and can offer no remedy to the illness secreted by a profit society.

Strive from your earliest years, my child, espouse the ends that society offers you, since its experience is millennial. Apply yourself to imitate others, ignore your own tastes and your vocation, be realistic. Your happiness consists in agreement. Be white or black, part of the majority or the opposition, you are free—but you must take sides and fight in the universal battle that will produce the common good; otherwise, you're a traitor and will be punished. In this way crowds are caught up in the rush to conformity. Lured by money and success, they become raw material for dictatorships, and for the democracies which are partly or already dictatorships. It sometimes happens that men decide to excel in order to institute reforms. They usually end up destroyed, content to mediate between various tendencies, to adjust appearances, to bring laws into line with customs. Others set out to be revolutionaries. But to employ violence against these evils is to bear them in oneself. As soon as a cause triumphs, it's time to oppose it in the very name of the values that created it.

My preference is for rebels, those whose sanity leads them to relativize the ideas and automatic reflexes that society produces in them. A rebel is not so reckless as to reject society, and will even bless it for its furnishings and the security it provides, despite all its blemishes. Its accomplishments are astounding—its roads, cities, and towers. If only they expressed the creative presence of the men and women of our time instead of being cathedrals of money.

The rebel is prejudiced in favor of a society that welcomes foreigners, the handicapped, wanderers, and all the parasites, which also permit it to breathe. As soon as it closes its doors to keep itself clean, to exclude others, to line up everyone in ranks, it's goodbye to innocence and humor. The rebel is on the side of the poor—those who aren't simply hoping to replace the rich—but don't expect the rebels to get aroused by electoral passions or be interested in the ideology of parties, even though they realize ideology is necessary. Rebels spontaneously see repetition in what is announced as different and they avoid false problems. They are troublemakers because they want neither to command nor to obey, and hence they are hard to catch. If only everyone would do the same! There are always enough people who will follow, and enough others, drawn by ambition, who will jump on the stage, scramble for power, and conceal their disappointment in love. They are our servants, assigned to the inhuman. We owe them respect.

We are too prone to blame everything on circumstances. They are in good part alibis. Modern society oppresses individuals so much only because they are spiritually empty and secretly applaud this oppression which, for better or worse, allows them to live from day to day.

The rebel is uninterested in ordinary purposes: growth, the standard of living, success, respectability. How could she feel guilty about this when she sees so many others passionately concerned about them, and with such high seriousness, finding them the only reason for existence? Her mission is to point to absence—it's not exactly her mission, more her nature. Amidst prophets who have become publicity agents, she invites us to make the world revolution in ourselves. Her only merit is to accept silence and solitude on days when she is tempted to quit. But no one should mistake her for an ascetic or a sage. I'm impressed that she seems to want almost nothing. She hardly dares to call herself Christian. Another word would be needed, more modest.

It's difficult to live both on the boundary and within. It presents a trap for the kind of person I'm describing. In order to resist incomprehension and scorn she is led either to withdraw into herself—with the result that she'll simply be considered a curiosity—or to harden herself and force her voice to denounce evil, forgetting that whatever rises up in her against society is also that which secretly is in league with it. In the same way, the prostitute dreams of her First Communion and of having a fashionable marriage in order to enter approved society. The gangster wants to end up a prominent businessman. Be suspicious of the rebel who uses her insurrection as stepladder.

Nevertheless, after she has contained herself a long time, watched out and kept her sense of humor, she may suddenly unleash all her resentment. The only societies that are real to her are small temporary societies within the huge social body. Temporary, because life is in transit. Fidelity is elsewhere.

Not that the rebel holds the secret of language or throws its sullied words in our face. Don't hold back what you discover. Surrender it that very instant. Empty wineskin, cymbal. If she possesses such knowledge, she is no longer anything but an actor who plays herself in some private drama. It's impossible to grow without dying. But don't wait until your final agony to become enlightened. Don't think I have come to bring peace (Mt 10), I have come to bring a sword. For I have come to divide a man from his father, a daughter from her mother, and a daughter-in-law from her mother-in-law, so that we will have the members of our own household as enemies.

Destroy prejudices, liberate yourself, liberate me. Throw stones at the mirrors of the palace of concepts and hike out into the friendly forests. I speak in images: I have no desire to change you into overage hippies. Since it's useless to cry out, smile at yourself, since you're not so brave every day.

If you hear someone speaking a language you were waiting for and which delights you, be on the alert. Is it a fake? Let me put you on guard against myself. But don't waste your time in being for or against. Let the almost nothing between the lines grow within you and take form.

Refuse to live only for work, money, the illusion of happiness, the distant future. Your sons will take care of themselves. They are no more important than those of the janitor. Therefore, reject efficiency at every price and any action that isn't meaningful to you. Give top priority to the decision to create a space and time for games, gratuitousness, the unexpected, for what can be neither bought nor sold, the instant: "enduring love." People don't decide to love, but if the way is cleared, love sometimes survives. These are suggestions which, without being necessarily Christian, are sufficiently in agreement with Christian experience.

It's harder than you think to prosper in society such as it is, to accept its ruling ideas, without participating in inhumanity. To pretend to live humanly or as a Christian is only a utopia or an illusion if we don't create favorable conditions. As soon as circumstances make it possible, try to break out. Earn less, resign. I'm not telling you to absent yourselves or be content with simply watching the caravan of sadness, but to be present differently. If you're caught in the daily round, let your anger build up: it's an indication of hope. You'll mark the calendar for a day when you'll be able to live according to your own rhythm. You'll have to be willing to lose respectability and all false social virtues, but you'll give joy to someone, to a few—and that's enough.

Solitude is not necessarily a retreat from communion. The deepening of subjectivity can be liberating for others. A day can come when you will belong totally to yourself—that is, to what created you, when alleluia breaks forth. Then you'll no longer want to wall yourself in, and in communion with all things you'll rejoin the universal in a vital experience. You will still sweat blood, but a tiny unshakable joy awaits you in every corner.

A few tips: Try to realize, without quite wanting to, that you are nothing, scarcely more than an earthworm, and through that experience become uncompromising. For it's impossible to go any lower. Therefore, be free in regard to conventions and other forms of sterility, whether accepting them provisionally or rejecting them. Don't take away anyone else's certitudes. Everything ripens in its time. Comfort yourselves with them, but know it, and smile at what happens.

When you see serious people acting as solemn as judges, tell them that they're looking at existence through the prism of their ideas. If it helps relieve your own sadness, think of them as fish in an aquarium.

Strangle the phrase with which you were going to compare the present with the past or fear for your future. Leap into the present instant; the past and the future are contained within it, and it carries its load of the eternal. Stop torturing yourself, poisoning your own life. Disappointed hopes, a broken heart—she has wounded me to death, he has destroyed me—what vanities these are! Happiness is not in happiness; it's in the unending process. Then let's get going, live as long as you're alive, do something, something absurd. Or better, who knows, if you've just had dinner, quietly do the dishes.